Learning and Developmental Disabilities SOURCEBOOK

SECOND EDITION

Disability Series

Learning and Developmental Disabilities SOURCEBOOK

SECOND EDITION

Basic Consumer Health Information about Developmental Milestones and Learning Disabilities; Their Causes, Signs, Diagnosis, and Treatment; Common Developmental Disorders That Affect Learning; as well as School and Career Options Accessible to Youth with Disabilities

Along with Resources Providing Support for Individuals with Learning and Developmental Disabilities

OMNIGRAPHICS
An imprint of Infobase

Bibliographic Note
Because this page cannot legibly accommodate all the copyright notices,
the Bibliographic Note portion of the Preface constitutes an extension
of the copyright notice.

* * *

OMNIGRAPHICS
An imprint of Infobase
8 The Green
Suite 19225
Dover, DE 19901
www.infobase.com
James Chambers, *Editorial Director*

* * *

Copyright © 2024 Infobase
ISBN 978-0-7808-2128-6
E-ISBN 978-0-7808-2129-3

Library of Congress Cataloging-in-Publication Data
Names: Chambers, James (Editor), editor.
Title: Learning and developmental disabilities sourcebook / James Chambers.
Description: Second edition. | Wilmington, DE: Omnigraphics, an imprint of Infobase, [2024] | Series: Disability series | Includes index. | Summary: "Provides consumer health information about the developmental milestones, types of learning disabilities, and developmental disorders that affect learning, along with effective strategies for providing support and promoting independence. Includes an index and resources for additional information"-- Provided by publisher.
Identifiers: LCCN 2024006376 (print) | LCCN 2024006377 (ebook) | ISBN 9780780821286 (library binding) | ISBN 9780780821293 (ebook)
Subjects: LCSH: Learning disabilities. | Learning disabled. | Developmental disabilities.
Classification: LCC LC4704 .L3766 2024 (print) | LCC LC4704 (ebook) | DDC 371.9--dc23/eng/20240215
LC record available at https://lccn.loc.gov/2024006376
LC ebook record available at https://lccn.loc.gov/2024006377

Electronic or mechanical reproduction, including photography, recording, or any other information storage and retrieval system for the purpose of resale is strictly prohibited without permission in writing from the publisher.

The information in this publication was compiled from the sources cited and from other sources considered reliable. While every possible effort has been made to ensure reliability, the publisher will not assume liability for damages caused by inaccuracies in the data, and makes no warranty, express or implied, on the accuracy of the information contained herein.

This book is printed on acid-free paper meeting the ANSI Z39.48 Standard. The infinity symbol that appears above indicates that the paper in this book meets that standard.

Printed in the United States

Table of Contents

Preface | ix

Part 1: Developmental Milestones and Learning Disabilities
Chapter 1—Understanding Developmental Milestones | 3
    Section 1.1—Early Cognitive Development | 4
    Section 1.2—Developmental Monitoring, Screening, and Evaluation | 7
    Section 1.3—Speech and Language Development | 10
Chapter 2—Early Influences on Brain Architecture and Learning | 13
Chapter 3—Understanding Learning Disability | 19
    Section 3.1—Types, Causes, and Signs of Learning Disability | 20
    Section 3.2—Diagnosing Learning Disability | 24

Part 2: Specific Types of Learning Disabilities
Chapter 4—Reading Disorders | 29
    Section 4.1—Reading Disability: An Overview | 30
    Section 4.2—Understanding Dyslexia | 33
Chapter 5—Dysgraphia | 37
Chapter 6—Dyscalculia | 41
Chapter 7—Learning Disability and Comorbid Conditions | 45
    Section 7.1—Language and Speech Disorders | 46
    Section 7.2—Specific Language Impairment | 49
    Section 7.3—Auditory Processing Disorder | 52
    Section 7.4—Visual Processing Disorders | 55
    Section 7.5—Developmental Dyspraxia | 59
    Section 7.6—Nonverbal Learning Disability | 62

Part 3: Common Developmental Disorders That Affect Learning
Chapter 8—Attention Deficit Hyperactivity Disorder | 69
Chapter 9—Autism Spectrum Disorder | 73
Chapter 10—Cerebral Palsy | 79
Chapter 11—Birth Defects and Intellectual Disability | 85
Chapter 12—Fetal Alcohol Spectrum Disorders | 91
Chapter 13—Hearing and Vision Loss | 97
Chapter 14—Genetic Disorders and Learning Disability | 103

Part 4: Providing Support and Promoting Independence
Chapter 15—Addressing Concerns about Child Development | 113
Chapter 16—Early Intervention Strategies | 117
Chapter 17—Educational Interventions | 127
Chapter 18—Special Education Process | 131
    Section 18.1—Steps in Special Education | 132
    Section 18.2—Individuals with Disabilities Education Act | 136
    Section 18.3—Guide to the Individualized Education Program | 138
Chapter 19—Support and Accommodations for Students | 143
Chapter 20—Preemployment Transition Services | 149
    Section 20.1—Vocational Rehabilitation Services | 150
    Section 20.2—Individualized Plan for Employment | 158
Chapter 21—Transition Planning and Programs | 163
    Section 21.1—Education and Training Opportunities in High School and Secondary School | 164
    Section 21.2—Planning for Out-of-School Youth | 171

Part 5: Living with Learning and Developmental Disabilities
Chapter 22—Transitioning to Adulthood | 175
    Section 22.1—Addressing Social and Emotional Needs | 176
    Section 22.2—Self-Determination for Youth with Disabilities | 179
    Section 22.3—Making Informed Choices | 183
Chapter 23—Career Options and Supported Employment | 187
    Section 23.1—Postsecondary Employment Options | 188
    Section 23.2—Intellectual Disability and the Americans with Disabilities Act | 193
Chapter 24—Philosophy of Independent Living | 201

Chapter 25—Sexuality, Relationships, and Disabilities | 205
        Section 25.1—Supporting Youth through Puberty
                and Adolescence | 206
        Section 25.2—Talking about Sexual Health | 210
        Section 25.3—Preventing and Responding to
                Sexual Abuse | 214

Part 6: Additional Resources

Chapter 26—Directory of Organizations Providing Support
        for People with Learning and Developmental
        Disabilities | 219

Index | 225

Preface

ABOUT THIS BOOK

Learning disabilities affect how individuals learn to read, write, speak, and comprehend math. These disabilities stem from differences in the brain function, occasionally involving structural variances. Often, individuals may experience more than one learning disability, but with appropriate educational support, they can still achieve success. In 2021–2022, approximately 7.3 million students aged 3–21 received special education or related services under the Individuals with Disabilities Education Act (IDEA), accounting for 15 percent of all public school students. Among these students, specific learning disabilities constituted the most prevalent category, affecting 32 percent.

Learning and Developmental Disabilities Sourcebook, Second Edition begins with an exploration of developmental milestones and diverse learning and developmental hurdles. It explains specific learning disabilities such as reading disorders, speech and language impairments (SLI), and nonverbal learning challenges. Furthermore, it examines prevalent developmental disorders such as cerebral palsy (CP), attention deficit hyperactivity disorder (ADHD), autism, and genetic conditions. Acknowledging the critical importance of support and self-reliance, it furnishes readers with management strategies, emphasizing resilience building in individuals facing these obstacles. As a comprehensive guide for families, educators, and professionals, it navigates the intricacies of aiding individuals with learning and developmental disabilities through early intervention, accommodations, transition planning, and independent living programs. The book concludes with a list of government organizations related to learning and developmental disabilities.

HOW TO USE THIS BOOK

This book is divided into parts and chapters. Parts focus on broad areas of interest; chapters are devoted to single topics within a part.

Part 1: Developmental Milestones and Learning Disabilities offers a foundational comprehension of developmental milestones and learning disabilities. It begins with an extensive examination of early cognitive development, developmental monitoring, and speech and language progression. It further explores how early life influences affect brain architecture and learning, concluding with a comprehensive discussion on the causes, signs, and diagnosis of learning disabilities.

Part 2: Specific Types of Learning Disabilities focuses on particular learning disabilities, exploring reading disorders such as dyslexia, dysgraphia, and dyscalculia. Additionally, it examines learning disabilities alongside coexisting conditions such as speech and language disorders, specific language impairment (SLI), auditory and visual processing disorders, developmental dyspraxia, and nonverbal learning disabilities (NVLD).

Part 3: Common Developmental Disorders That Affect Learning explains diverse developmental disorders that affect learning and cognitive abilities. It covers a range of conditions such as birth defects, intellectual disabilities, attention deficit hyperactivity disorder (ADHD), autism spectrum disorder (ASD), cerebral palsy (CP), fetal alcohol spectrum disorders (FASDs), and genetic disorders, focusing on understanding these conditions and their interplay with learning disabilities.

Part 4: Providing Support and Promoting Independence addresses concerns regarding child development and offers insights into early intervention strategies. It outlines support mechanisms and methods for promoting independence, including educational interventions, special education processes, supports, and accommodations for students. Additionally, it covers preemployment transition services and transition planning and programs, providing comprehensive guidance for educators, parents, and caregivers.

Part 5: Living with Learning and Developmental Disabilities explores the comprehensive experience of living with such conditions. It focuses on transitioning to adulthood, career opportunities, the philosophy of independent living, and aspects of sexuality and relationships. It also provides an in-depth examination of the Developmental Disabilities Assistance and Bill of Rights Act, emphasizing legal rights and support structures.

Part 6: Additional Resources includes a list of government organizations related to learning and developmental disabilities.

BIBLIOGRAPHIC NOTE

This volume contains documents and excerpts from publications issued by the following U.S. government agencies: Administration for Children and Families (ACF); Center for Parent Information & Resources (CPIR); ChildCare.gov; Early Childhood Learning and Knowledge Center (ECLKC); *Eunice Kennedy Shriver* National Institute of Child Health and Human Development (NICHD); MedlinePlus; National Center on Birth Defects and Developmental Disabilities (NCBDDD); National Human Genome Research Institute (NHGRI); National Institute of Mental Health (NIMH); National Institute of Neurological Disorders and Stroke (NINDS); National Institute on Deafness and Other Communication Disorders (NIDCD); *NIH News in Health*; Office of Disease Prevention and Health Promotion (ODPHP); U.S. Department of Education (ED); U.S. Equal Employment Opportunity Commission (EEOC); and Youth.gov.

It also contains original material produced by Infobase.

MEDICAL REVIEW

Infobase works with a staff subject matter expert, Dr. Naveen Sundararaj, who consults on and reviews all original articles written for the *Disability Series* to ensure currency and accuracy.

ABOUT THE *DISABILITY SERIES*

At the request of librarians serving the one in four Americans living with a disability, as well as those seeking information to comprehend, navigate, and manage such conditions, the *Disability Series* was developed as a specialized collection within Omnigraphics' *Health Reference Series*. Each volume comprehensively addresses a specific topic chosen based on the needs and interests of these patrons. These volumes offer authoritative health information, serving as a reliable resource for librarians to equip consumers with the necessary facts to take charge of their well-being. This empowers individuals to better understand and address health challenges faced by themselves, family members, or loved ones. Patrons in search of this information can find answers in the *Disability Series*. The *Series*, however, is not designed for diagnosing disabilities, prescribing treatments, or substituting the health-care provider-patient relationship. Anyone concerned about medical symptoms, the potential for disability, or illness is encouraged to seek professional care from an appropriate health-care provider.

If you have suggestions for future *Disability Series* topics, please email us at: custserv@infobaselearning.com.

A NOTE ABOUT SPELLING AND STYLE

Disability Series editors use *Stedman's Medical Dictionary* as an authority for questions related to the spelling of medical terms and *The Chicago Manual of Style* for questions related to grammatical structures, punctuation, and other editorial concerns. Consistent adherence is not always possible, however, because the individual volumes within the *Series* include many documents from a wide variety of different producers, and the editor's primary goal is to present material from each source as accurately as is possible. This sometimes means that information in different chapters or sections may follow other guidelines and alternate spelling authorities. For example, occasionally a copyright holder may require that eponymous terms be shown in possessive forms (Crohn's disease vs. Crohn disease) or that British spelling norms be retained (leukaemia vs. leukemia).

Part 1 | Developmental Milestones and Learning Disabilities

Chapter 1 | Understanding Developmental Milestones

Chapter Contents

Section 1.1—Early Cognitive Development 4

Section 1.2—Developmental Monitoring, Screening, and Evaluation 7

Section 1.3—Speech and Language Development 10

Section 1.1 | Early Cognitive Development

Early childhood, particularly the first five years of life, affects long-term social, cognitive, emotional, and physical development. Healthy development in early childhood helps prepare children for the educational experiences of kindergarten and beyond. Early childhood development and education opportunities are affected by various environmental and social factors, including early life stress, socioeconomic status, relationships with parents and caregivers, and access to early education programs.[1]

Children play an active role in their own cognitive development by exploring and testing the world around them, but they also need support from parents, teachers, and other adults. When infants and toddlers feel safe and secure, they are more willing to experiment with their world, such as discovering how a pull toy works, observing what happens when they turn on a faucet, and trying out different behaviors to see how people react. In the process, they begin to understand basic mathematical, spatial, and causal relationships. Toddlers also explore concepts through a variety of symbolic activities, such as drawing and pretend play. More and more, young children can rely on their developing memory to help them make sense of the world. All this activity in the first three years lays the foundation for the more complex cognitive skills that preschoolers develop.

DOMAINS OF COGNITIVE DEVELOPMENT

Cognitive development is presented as two different domains for preschoolers—mathematics development and scientific reasoning—to reflect the increasingly complex and more differentiated cognitive abilities of this age period. Mathematics development in preschoolers refers to understanding numbers and quantities, their relationships, and operations, such as what it means to add to and take away. Mathematics also includes shapes and their structure, reasoning, measurement, classification, and patterns. Preschoolers

---

[1] Office of Disease Prevention and Health Promotion (ODPHP), "Early Childhood Development and Education," U.S. Department of Health and Human Services (HHS), August 7, 2022. Available online. URL: https://health.gov/healthypeople/priority-areas/social-determinants-health/literature-summaries/early-childhood-development-and-education. Accessed February 2, 2024.

are eager to measure their height to see how much they have grown and to chime in with repeating patterns in books and songs.

Increasingly, children use math strategies to solve problems during daily activities, such as figuring out how many more cups are needed at snack time. Because math includes generalizations and abstractions, math skills help young children connect ideas, develop logical and abstract thinking, and analyze, question, and understand the world around them. Children develop math concepts and skills through active exploration and discovery in the context of stimulating learning opportunities and intentional teaching strategies.

Scientific reasoning refers to the emerging ability to develop scientific knowledge about the natural and physical worlds, learn scientific skills and methods, and continue developing reasoning and problem-solving skills. For preschoolers, scientific investigation includes making observations, recording them, talking about them, and analyzing them. Their investigations reflect their natural interests in how things work in plants and animals, their bodies, and the weather. In the process of investigating, they can learn to use measurement and observational tools, such as a ruler and a magnifying glass. During the early childhood years, science provides opportunities for rich vocabulary learning and collaboration with peers and fosters a sense of curiosity and motivation to learn. Problem-solving and reasoning become more complex as preschoolers gain new abilities to ask questions and gather information.

Because cognitive development encompasses a broad range of skills, behaviors, and concepts, children display great individual variation in their development from birth to five years of age. Prior experiences, cultural and linguistic backgrounds, temperament, and many other factors can affect the rate and course of cognitive development. Children with disabilities may require extra support as they use their senses and bodies to explore or as they describe their scientific investigations. The instruction and learning opportunities young children experience set the stage for their cognitive development and success.[2]

---

[2] "Interactive Head Start Early Learning Outcomes Framework: Ages Birth to Five," Early Childhood Learning and Knowledge Center (ECLKC), September 20, 2015. Available online. URL: https://eclkc.ohs.acf.hhs.gov/interactive-head-start-early-learning-outcomes-framework-ages-birth-five. Accessed February 2, 2024.

EARLY DEVELOPMENTAL MILESTONES

Infants (Zero to One Year of Age)

Skills such as taking a first step, smiling for the first time, and waving "bye-bye" are called "developmental milestones." Developmental milestones are things most children can do by a certain age. Children reach milestones in how they play, learn, speak, behave, and move (such as crawling, walking, or jumping).

In the first year, babies learn to focus their vision, reach out, explore, and learn about the things that are around them. Cognitive, or brain development, means the learning process of memory, language, thinking, and reasoning. Learning language is more than making sounds ("babble") or saying "mama" and "dada." Listening, understanding, and knowing the names of people and things are all a part of language development. During this stage, babies also develop bonds of love and trust with their parents and others as part of social and emotional development.

Toddlers (One to Two Years of Age)

During the second year, toddlers move around more and are aware of themselves and their surroundings. Their desire to explore new objects and people is also increasing. During this stage, toddlers will show greater independence, begin to show defiant behavior, recognize themselves in pictures or a mirror, and imitate the behavior of others, especially adults and older children. Toddlers should also be able to recognize the names of familiar people and objects, form simple phrases and sentences, and follow simple instructions and directions.

Toddlers (Two to Three Years of Age)

Skills such as taking turns, playing make-believe, and kicking a ball are called "developmental milestones." Toddlers will experience huge thinking, learning, social, and emotional changes that will help them explore their new world and make sense of it. During this stage, toddlers should be able to follow two- or three-step directions, sort objects by shape and color, imitate the actions of adults and playmates, and express a wide range of emotions.

Preschoolers (Three to Five Years of Age)

Skills such as naming colors, showing affection, and hopping on one foot are called "developmental milestones." As children grow into early childhood, their world will begin to open up. They will become more independent and begin to focus more on adults and children outside of the family. They will want to explore and ask about the things around them even more. Their interactions with family and those around them will help shape their personality and their own ways of thinking and moving. During this stage, children should be able to ride a tricycle, use safety scissors, notice a difference between girls and boys, help dress and undress themselves, play with other children, recall part of a story, and sing a song.[3]

Section 1.2 | Developmental Monitoring, Screening, and Evaluation

Many children with developmental delays or behavior concerns are not identified as early as possible. As a result, these children must wait to get the help they need to do well in social and educational settings (e.g., in school, at home, and in the community).

DEVELOPMENTAL MONITORING

Developmental monitoring observes how your child grows and changes over time and whether your child meets the typical developmental milestones in playing, learning, speaking, behaving, and moving. Parents, grandparents, early childhood providers, and other caregivers can participate in developmental monitoring. If you notice that your child is not meeting milestones, talk with your doctor or nurse about your concerns.

When you take your child to a well-child visit, your doctor or nurse will also do developmental monitoring. The doctor or nurse

---

[3] National Center on Birth Defects and Developmental Disabilities (NCBDDD), "Infants (0–1 Year of Age)," Centers for Disease Control and Prevention (CDC), November 29, 2021. Available online. URL: www.cdc.gov/ncbddd/childdevelopment/positiveparenting/infants.html. Accessed February 2, 2024.

might ask you questions about your child's development or will talk and play with your child to see if he or she is developing and meeting milestones. A missed milestone could be a sign of a problem, so the doctor or another specialist will take a closer look by using a more thorough test or exam.

DEVELOPMENTAL SCREENING

Developmental screening takes a closer look at how your child is developing. Your child will get a brief test, or you will complete a questionnaire about your child. The tools used for developmental and behavioral screening are formal questionnaires or checklists based on research that ask questions about a child's development, including language, movement, thinking, behavior, and emotions. Developmental screening can be done not only by a doctor or nurse but also by other professionals in health care, early childhood education, community, or school settings.

Developmental screening is more formal than developmental monitoring and is normally done less often than developmental monitoring. Your child should be screened if you or your doctor has a concern. However, developmental screening is a regular part of some of the well-child visits for all children even if there is not a known concern.

The American Academy of Pediatrics (AAP) recommends developmental and behavioral screening for all children during regular well-child visits at the following ages:

- 9 months
- 18 months
- 30 months

In addition, the AAP recommends that all children be screened specifically for autism spectrum disorder (ASD) during regular well-child visits at:

- 18 months
- 24 months

If your child is at higher risk for developmental concerns due to preterm birth, low birth weight, environmental risks such as lead exposure, or other factors, your health-care provider may also discuss additional screening. If a child has an existing long-lasting

Understanding Developmental Milestones | 9

health concern or a diagnosed condition, the child should have developmental monitoring and screening in all areas of development, just like those without special health-care needs.

If your child's health-care provider does not periodically check your child with a developmental screening test, you can ask that it be done.

DEVELOPMENTAL EVALUATION

A brief test using a screening tool does not provide a diagnosis, but it indicates if a child is on the right development track or if a specialist should take a closer look. If the screening tool identifies an area of concern, a formal developmental evaluation may be needed. This formal evaluation is a more in-depth look at a child's development, usually done by a trained specialist, such as a developmental pediatrician, child psychologist, speech-language pathologist, occupational therapist, physical therapist, or other specialist. The specialist may observe the child, give the child a structured test, ask the parents or caregivers questions, or ask them to fill out questionnaires. The results of this formal evaluation determine whether a child needs special treatments, early intervention services, or both.

Facts about Developmental Monitoring
- **Who**. You—parents, grandparents, or other caregivers.
- **What**. To look for developmental milestones.
- **When**. From birth to five years of age.
- **Why**. To help you:
  - celebrate your child's development
  - talk about your child's progress with doctors and child-care providers
  - learn what to expect next
  - identify any concerns early
- **How**. With easy, free checklists available at www.cdc.gov/Milestones.

Facts about Developmental Screening
- **Who**. Health-care provider, early childhood teacher, or other trained provider.

- **What**. To look for developmental milestones.
- **When**:
  - developmental screening at 9, 18, and 30 months of age
  - autism screening at 18 and 24 months of age
- **Why**. To find out:
  - if your child needs more help with development because it is not always obvious to doctors, childcare providers, or parents
  - if more developmental evaluations are recommended
- **How**. With a formal, validated screening tool available at www.acf.hhs.gov/archive/ecd/child-health-development/watch-me-thrive.

Facts about Developmental Evaluation
- **Who**. Developmental pediatrician, child psychologist, or other trained provider.
- **What**. To identify and diagnose developmental delays and conditions.
- **When**. Whenever there is a concern.
- **Why**. To find out:
  - if your child needs specific treatment
  - if your child qualifies for early intervention
- **How**. With a detailed examination, formal assessment tools, observation, and surveys from parents and other caregivers, often in combination, depending on the area of concern.[4]

Section 1.3 | Speech and Language Development

WHAT ARE VOICE, SPEECH, AND LANGUAGE?
Voice, speech, and language are the tools we use to communicate with each other.

---

[4] National Center on Birth Defects and Developmental Disabilities (NCBDDD), "Developmental Monitoring and Screening," Centers for Disease Control and Prevention (CDC), April 13, 2023. Available online. URL: www.cdc.gov/ncbddd/childdevelopment/screening.html. Accessed February 2, 2024.

- **Voice.** This is the sound we make as air from our lungs is pushed between vocal folds in our larynx, causing them to vibrate.
- **Speech.** This is talking, which is one way to express language. It involves the precisely coordinated muscle actions of the tongue, lips, jaw, and vocal tract to produce the recognizable sounds that make up language.
- **Language.** This is a set of shared rules that allow people to express their ideas in a meaningful way. Language may be expressed verbally or by writing, signing, or making other gestures, such as eye blinking or mouth movements.

HOW DO SPEECH AND LANGUAGE DEVELOP?

The first three years of life, when the brain is developing and maturing, is the most intensive period for acquiring speech and language skills. These skills develop best in a world that is rich with sounds, sights, and consistent exposure to the speech and language of others. There appear to be critical periods for speech and language development in infants and young children when the brain is best able to absorb language. If these critical periods are allowed to pass without exposure to language, it will be more difficult to learn.

WHAT ARE THE MILESTONES FOR SPEECH AND LANGUAGE DEVELOPMENT?

The first signs of communication occur when an infant learns that a cry will bring food, comfort, and companionship. Newborns also begin to recognize important sounds in their environment, such as the voice of their mother or primary caretaker. As they grow, babies begin to sort out the speech sounds that compose the words of their language. By six months of age, most babies recognize the basic sounds of their native language.

Children vary in their development of speech and language skills. However, they follow a natural progression or timetable for mastering the skills of language. These milestones help doctors and other health professionals determine if a child is on track or if he or she may need extra help. Sometimes a delay may be caused by hearing loss, while other times, it may be due to a speech or language disorder.

WHAT IS THE DIFFERENCE BETWEEN A SPEECH DISORDER AND A LANGUAGE DISORDER?

Children who have trouble understanding what others say (receptive language) or difficulty sharing their thoughts (expressive language) may have a language disorder. Developmental language disorder (DLD) is a language disorder that delays the mastery of language skills. Some children with DLD may not begin to talk until their third or fourth year. Children who have trouble producing speech sounds correctly or who hesitate or stutter when talking may have a speech disorder. Apraxia of speech (AOS) is a speech disorder that makes it difficult to put sounds and syllables together in the correct order to form words.

WHAT SHOULD YOU DO IF YOUR CHILD'S SPEECH OR LANGUAGE APPEARS TO BE DELAYED?

Talk to your child's doctor if you have any concerns. Your doctor may refer you to a speech-language pathologist, who is a health professional trained to evaluate and treat people with speech or language disorders. The speech-language pathologist will talk to you about your child's communication and general development. He or she will also use special spoken tests to evaluate your child. A hearing test is often included in the evaluation because a hearing problem can affect speech and language development. Depending on the result of the evaluation, the speech-language pathologist may suggest activities you can do at home to stimulate your child's development. They might also recommend a group or individual therapy or suggest further evaluation by an audiologist (a health-care professional trained to identify and measure hearing loss) or a developmental psychologist (a health-care professional with special expertise in the psychological development of infants and children).[5]

---

[5] "Speech and Language Developmental Milestones," National Institute on Deafness and Other Communication Disorders (NIDCD), October 13, 2022. Available online. URL: www.nidcd.nih.gov/health/speech-and-language. Accessed February 2, 2024.

Chapter 2 | Early Influences on Brain Architecture and Learning

EARLY BRAIN DEVELOPMENT AND HEALTH

The early years of a child's life are very important for later health and development. One of the main reasons is how fast the brain grows, starting before birth and continuing into early childhood. Although the brain continues to develop and change into adulthood, the first eight years can build a foundation for future learning, health, and life success. How well a brain develops depends on many factors in addition to genes, such as:
- proper nutrition starting in pregnancy
- exposure to toxins or infections
- the child's experiences with other people and the world

Nurturing and responsive care for the child's body and mind is the key to supporting healthy brain development. Positive or negative experiences can add up to shape a child's development and can have lifelong effects. To nurture their child's body and mind, parents and caregivers need support and the right resources. The right care for children, starting before birth and continuing through childhood, ensures that the child's brain grows well and reaches its full potential.

THE IMPORTANCE OF EARLY CHILDHOOD EXPERIENCES FOR BRAIN DEVELOPMENT

Children are born ready to learn and have many skills to learn over many years. They depend on parents, family members, and other caregivers as their first teachers to develop the right skills to become independent and lead healthy and successful lives. How the brain grows is strongly affected by the child's experiences with other people and the world. Nurturing care for the mind is critical for brain growth. Children grow and learn best in a safe environment where they are protected from neglect and from extreme or chronic stress with plenty of opportunities to play and explore.

Parents and other caregivers can support healthy brain growth by speaking to, playing with, and caring for their child. Children learn best when parents take turns when talking and playing and build on their child's skills and interests. Nurturing a child by understanding their needs and responding sensitively helps protect children's brains from stress. Speaking with children and exposing them to books, stories, and songs help strengthen children's language and communication, which puts them on a path toward learning and succeeding in school.

Exposure to stress and trauma can have long-term negative consequences for the child's brain, whereas talking, reading, and playing can stimulate brain growth. Ensuring that parents, caregivers, and early childhood care providers have the resources and skills to provide safe, stable, nurturing, and stimulating care is an important public health goal. When children are at risk, tracking children's development and making sure they reach developmental milestones can help ensure that any problems are detected early and children can receive the intervention they may need.

A HEALTHY START FOR THE BRAIN

To learn and grow appropriately, a baby's brain has to be healthy and protected from diseases and other risks. Promoting the development of a healthy brain can start even before pregnancy. For example, a healthy diet and the right nutrients, such as sufficient folic acid, will promote a healthy pregnancy and a healthy nervous system in the growing baby. Vaccinations can protect pregnant women from infections that can harm the brain of the unborn baby.

During pregnancy, the brain can be affected by many types of risks, such as by infectious diseases such as cytomegalovirus (CMV) or Zika virus; by exposure to toxins, including from smoking or alcohol; or when pregnant mothers experience stress, trauma, or mental health conditions such as depression. Regular health care during pregnancy can help prevent complications, including premature birth, which can affect the baby's brain. Newborn screening can detect conditions that are potentially dangerous to the child's brain, such as phenylketonuria (PKU).

Healthy brain growth in infancy continues to depend on the right care and nutrition. Because children's brains are still growing, they are especially vulnerable to traumatic head injuries, infections, or toxins, such as lead. Childhood vaccines, such as the measles vaccine, can protect children from dangerous complications such as swelling of the brain. Ensuring that parents and caregivers have access to healthy foods and places to live and play that are healthy and safe for their children can help them provide more nurturing care.[1]

BRAIN DEVELOPMENT

Science has shown that the relationships with the important people in a baby's life literally shape and form the architecture of the infant's brain. Deceptively simple, moment-to-moment interactions with responsive caregivers build the brain, creating or strengthening one connection at a time. By the time children are two years old, the structures of their brains that will influence later learning are mostly formed. This means that the most important brain growth and development, the kind that will physically form the brain, begins long before a child ever picks up a pencil, reads a book, or goes to school.

BUILDING CONNECTIONS

Although the brain looks like a gray blob, it is, in fact, made up of billions of cells called "neurons" that make electrical connections with each other. Each new experience or each piece of information releases chemicals called "hormones" that create a new connection,

---

[1] National Center on Birth Defects and Developmental Disabilities (NCBDDD), "Early Brain Development and Health," Centers for Disease Control and Prevention (CDC), February 24, 2023. Available online. URL: www.cdc.gov/ncbddd/childdevelopment/early-brain-development.html. Accessed February 12, 2024.

or synapse, in the brain. More connections are formed in the brain prenatally and in the first few years of life than at any other time. After early childhood, the connections that are not used as frequently will be pruned, or removed, to allow for more useful connections to grow stronger. Sometimes this process is referred to as "use it or lose it" since the parts of your brain you use the most become stronger while the parts you use less die off.

Two-month-old Elijah is crying. His father, Daniel, goes to him and says, "Ohh, what's going on, little one?" When Elijah sees his father's face and hears his voice, he immediately begins to calm down. At two months old, he already knows that when he cries, his father responds.

For newborns and young infants, most of their emotional experiences happen in moments of interaction with their caregivers. Newborn and caregiver interactions usually occur around activities such as comforting, feeding, and holding. As Elijah is calmed, hormones are released that help him be more alert and able to learn. The synapses in the brain that respond to and expect caring behavior from others will grow strong. This allows Elijah to feel safe and fully able to learn about the many interesting things in the world. Repeated over and over again during Elijah's first years of life, moments such as these will build the neural connections that will support learning for the rest of his life.

SERVE-AND-RETURN LEARNING

Two-month-old Amelia begins a "conversation" with her mother. She babbles, makes faces and gestures, and eventually cries when she has had enough. Her mother responds by echoing the sounds she makes, mirroring her facial expressions, and comforting her when she cries.

Thirteen-month-old Ethan brings his teacher a toy tiger. He hands her the tiger, and she says, "Thank you." Ethan then holds his hand out, and she gives the tiger back. He says, "Da du." They repeat this exchange half a dozen times before Ethan goes to find a new toy, and they start again.

Thirty-month-old Miguel is playing in the backyard. When he reaches the crest of a small hill, he turns to his family childcare provider and shouts, "Look at me!!" She looks at him and says, "You climbed to the top of the hill. Now what will you do?" He grins and says, "Roll!" After he rolls down the hill, he runs to her and touches her shoulder. She smiles at him, and he runs off again.

These vignettes illustrate typical interactions throughout the day of an infant or toddler. Each vignette provides an example of a common quality in relationships that is often repeated over and over again called "serve" and "return." Although the kind of exchanges that occur might be different depending on a child's age, each infant or toddler reaches out to a trusted adult who then responds. The adult's response acknowledges the child's intention or need and also encourages further interactions. Amelia is only two months old, yet she is able to engage her mother's attention, bring out her mother's smile, and elicit comfort. Ethan is engaged in a give-and-take game with his teacher. Miguel is much more independent but still checks with his caregiver as a secure base. These serve-and-return interactions build and strengthen neural connections that support feelings of safety and being an effective communicator. These strong connections build a foundation for all later learning.

TOXIC STRESS AND THE BRAIN

Jonah, a two-year-old who grew up in a chronically stressful environment, is playing with some blocks. Aiden comes over to join his play. As Aiden picks up a block, Jonah reacts impulsively by hitting and attempting to bite Aiden. The strongest connections in Jonah's brain, those that warn him of danger, react first. He strikes Aiden to protect himself and his belongings.

When infants and toddlers are regularly ignored, frequently experience violence, or spend much of their time in highly stressful environments, they are considered to be exposed to toxic stress. While normal life stressors are not dangerous and can even be healthy for a developing brain, toxic stress occurs when the body's response system to stress is activated much of the time. Our bodies produce a hormone called "cortisol" as part of the natural reaction to stress. In moderation, cortisol can contribute to a healthy brain structure. In extreme situations where a young child is feeling stressed much of the time, constant exposure to cortisol can alter the way the brain might otherwise develop. For example, a baby exposed to chronic stress is more likely to develop strong connections in the areas of their brain that are on alert for danger. Their brains may expect the world to be a dangerous place. When these babies are older, their brains interpret neutral events as more negative. When they become children and adults, their brains may spend more energy figuring out if they are in danger and have less attention for things their peers are focused on and learning.

The great news is that you can reduce the effect of toxic stress experienced by babies and young children. The loving, nurturing relationship that parents, family members, and teachers provide can act as a buffer to the effects of toxic stress. Consistent adult support can help a young child come through such difficulties with a brain that is still fully able to learn.[2]

---

[2] "Early Experiences Build the Brain," Early Childhood Learning and Knowledge Center (ECLKC), October 19, 2023. Available online. URL: https://eclkc.ohs.acf.hhs.gov/school-readiness/article/early-experiences-build-brain. Accessed February 12, 2024.

Chapter 3 | Understanding Learning Disability

Chapter Contents
Section 3.1—Types, Causes, and Signs of Learning Disability 20
Section 3.2—Diagnosing Learning Disability 24

Section 3.1 | Types, Causes, and Signs of Learning Disability

Learning disabilities affect how a person learns to read, write, speak, and do math. They are caused by differences in the brain, most often in how it functions but also sometimes in its structure. These differences affect the way the brain processes information. Learning disabilities are often discovered once a child is in school and has learning difficulties that do not improve over time. A person can have more than one learning disability. Learning disabilities can last a person's entire life, but he or she can still be successful with the right educational support. A learning disability is not an indication of a person's intelligence. Learning disabilities are different from learning problems due to intellectual and developmental disabilities (IDDs) or emotional, vision, hearing, or motor skills problems.

TYPES OF LEARNING DISABILITIES
Some of the most common learning disabilities are as follows:
- **Dyslexia**. People with dyslexia have problems with reading words accurately and with ease (sometimes called "fluency") and may have a hard time spelling, understanding sentences, and recognizing words they already know.
- **Dysgraphia**. People with dysgraphia have problems with their handwriting. They may have trouble forming letters, writing within a defined space, and writing down their thoughts.
- **Dyscalculia**. People with this math learning disability may have difficulty understanding arithmetic concepts and doing addition, multiplication, and measuring.
- **Apraxia of speech (AOS)**. This disorder involves problems with speaking. People with this disorder have trouble saying what they want to say. It is sometimes called "verbal apraxia."
- **Central auditory processing disorder**. People with this condition have trouble understanding and remembering language-related tasks. They have difficulty explaining things, understanding jokes, and following directions. They confuse words and are easily distracted.

- **Nonverbal learning disorder.** People with these conditions have strong verbal skills but difficulty understanding facial expressions and body language. They are clumsy and have trouble generalizing and following multistep directions.

Because there are many different types of learning disabilities and some people may have more than one, it is hard to estimate how many people might have learning disabilities.

WHAT CAUSES LEARNING DISABILITIES?

Researchers do not know all of the possible causes of learning disabilities, but they have found a range of risk factors during their work to find potential causes. Research shows that risk factors may be present from birth and tend to run in families. Children who have a parent with a learning disability are more likely to develop a learning disability themselves. To better understand learning disabilities, researchers are studying how children's brains learn to read, write, and develop math skills. Researchers are working on interventions to help address the needs of those who struggle with reading the most, including those with learning disabilities, to improve learning and overall health.

Factors that affect a fetus's development in the womb, such as alcohol or drug use, can put a child at higher risk for a learning problem or disability. Other factors in an infant's environment may play a role, too. These can include poor nutrition or exposure to lead in water or in paint. Young children who do not receive the support they need for their intellectual development may show signs of learning disabilities once they start school. Sometimes a person may develop a learning disability later in life due to injury. Possible causes in such a case include dementia or a traumatic brain injury (TBI).

SIGNS OF LEARNING DISABILITIES

Many children have trouble reading, writing, or performing other learning-related tasks at some point. This does not mean they have learning disabilities. A child with a learning disability often has several related signs, and they do not go away or get better over time. The signs of learning disabilities vary from person to person.

Common signs that a person may have learning disabilities include the following:
- problems reading and/or writing
- problems with math
- poor memory
- problems paying attention
- trouble following directions
- clumsiness
- trouble telling time
- problems staying organized

A child with a learning disability may also have one or more of the following:
- acting without really thinking about possible outcomes (impulsiveness)
- "acting out" in school or social situations
- difficulty staying focused or being easily distracted
- difficulty saying a word correctly out loud or expressing thoughts
- problems with school performance from week to week or from day to day
- speaking like a younger child; using short, simple phrases; or leaving out words in sentences
- having a hard time listening
- problems dealing with changes in schedule or situations
- problems understanding words or concepts

These signs alone are not enough to determine that a person has a learning disability. Only a professional can diagnose a learning disability. Each learning disability has its own signs. A person with a particular disability may not have all of the signs of that disability.

Children being taught in a second language may show signs of learning problems or a learning disability. The learning disability assessment must take into account whether a student is bilingual or a second-language learner. In addition, for English-speaking children, the assessment should be sensitive to differences that may be due to dialect, a form of a language that is specific to a region or group. The following are some common learning disabilities and the signs associated with them.

Dyslexia

People with dyslexia usually have trouble making the connection between letters and sounds and with spelling and recognizing words. People with dyslexia often show other signs of the condition. These may include the following:
- having a hard time understanding what others are saying
- difficulty organizing written and spoken language
- delay in being able to speak
- difficulty expressing thoughts or feelings
- difficulty learning new words (vocabulary) while either reading or hearing
- trouble learning foreign languages
- difficulty learning songs and rhymes
- slow rate of reading, both silently and out loud
- giving up on longer reading tasks
- difficulty understanding questions and following directions
- poor spelling
- problems remembering numbers in sequence (e.g., telephone numbers and addresses)
- trouble telling left from right

Dysgraphia

A child who has trouble writing or has very poor handwriting and does not outgrow it may have dysgraphia. This disorder may cause a child to be tense and twist awkwardly when holding a pen or pencil. Other signs of this condition may include the following:
- a strong dislike of writing and/or drawing
- problems with grammar
- trouble writing down ideas
- losing energy or interest as soon as they start writing
- trouble writing down thoughts in a logical sequence
- saying words out loud while writing
- leaving words unfinished or omitting them when writing sentences

Dyscalculia

Signs of this disability include problems understanding basic arithmetic concepts, such as fractions, number lines, and positive and negative numbers. Other symptoms may include the following:
- difficulty with math-related word problems
- trouble making a change in cash transactions
- messiness in putting math problems on paper
- trouble with logical sequences (e.g., steps in math problems)
- trouble understanding the time sequence of events
- trouble describing math processes[1]

Section 3.2 | Diagnosing Learning Disability

Learning disabilities are often identified once a child is in school. The school may use a process called "response to intervention" (RTI) to help identify children with learning disabilities. Special tests are required to make a diagnosis.

RESPONSE TO INTERVENTION

Response to intervention usually involves the following:
- monitoring all students' progress closely to identify possible learning problems
- providing children who are having problems with help on different levels or tiers
- moving children to tiers that provide increasing support if they do not show sufficient progress

Students who are struggling in school can also have individual evaluations. An evaluation can:
- identify whether a child has a learning disability
- determine a child's eligibility under federal law for special education services

---

[1] "Learning Disabilities," *Eunice Kennedy Shriver* National Institute of Child Health and Human Development (NICHD), September 11, 2018. Available online. URL: www.nichd.nih.gov/health/topics/learningdisabilities. Accessed February 6, 2024.

- help develop an Individualized Education Plan (IEP) that outlines help for a child who qualifies for special education services
- establish benchmarks to measure the child's progress

A full evaluation for a learning disability includes the following:
- a medical exam, including a neurological exam, to rule out other possible causes of the child's difficulties (These might include emotional disorders, intellectual and developmental disabilities (IDDs), and brain diseases.)
- reviewing the child's developmental, social, and school performance
- a discussion of family history
- academic and psychological testing

Usually, several specialists work as a team to do the evaluation. The team may include a psychologist, a special education expert, and a speech-language pathologist. Many schools also have reading specialists who can help diagnose a reading disability.

ROLE OF SCHOOL PSYCHOLOGISTS

School psychologists are trained in both education and psychology. They can help diagnose students with learning disabilities and help the student and his or her parents and teachers come up with plans to improve learning.

ROLE OF SPEECH-LANGUAGE PATHOLOGISTS

All speech-language pathologists are trained to diagnose and treat speech and language disorders. A speech-language pathologist can do a language evaluation and assess the child's ability to organize his or her thoughts and possessions. The speech-language pathologist may evaluate the child's learning skills, such as understanding directions, manipulating sounds, and reading and writing.[2]

---

[2] "How Are Learning Disabilities Diagnosed?" *Eunice Kennedy Shriver* National Institute of Child Health and Human Development (NICHD), September 11, 2018. Available online. URL: www.nichd.nih.gov/health/topics/learning/conditioninfo/diagnosed. Accessed February 5, 2024.

Part 2 | Specific Types of Learning Disabilities

Chapter 4 | Reading Disorders

Chapter Contents
Section 4.1—Reading Disability: An Overview 30
Section 4.2—Understanding Dyslexia 33

Section 4.1 | Reading Disability: An Overview

WHAT ARE READING DISORDERS?

Reading disorders occur when a person has trouble reading words or understanding what they read. Dyslexia is one type of reading disorder. It generally refers to difficulties reading individual words and can lead to problems understanding text. Most reading disorders result from specific differences in the way the brain processes written words and text. Usually, these differences are present from a young age. But a person can develop a reading problem from an injury to the brain at any age. People with reading disorders often have problems recognizing words they already know and understanding the text they read. They may also be poor spellers. Not everyone with a reading disorder has every symptom. Reading disorders are not a type of intellectual or developmental disorder, and they are not a sign of lower intelligence or unwillingness to learn. People with reading disorders may have other learning disabilities, too, including problems with writing or numbers.

TYPES OF READING DISORDERS

Dyslexia is the most well-known reading disorder. It specifically impairs a person's ability to read. Individuals with dyslexia have normal intelligence, but they read at levels significantly lower than expected. Although the disorder varies from person to person, there are common characteristics: People with dyslexia often have a hard time sounding out words, understanding written words, and naming objects quickly. Most reading problems are present from the time a child learns to read. However, some people lose the ability to read after a stroke or an injury to the area of the brain involved with reading. This kind of reading disorder is called "alexia."

Hyperlexia is a disorder where people have advanced reading skills but may have problems understanding what is read or spoken aloud. They may also have cognitive or social problems. Other people may have normal reading skills but have problems

understanding written words. Reading disorders can also involve problems with specific skills:
- **Word decoding.** People who have difficulty sounding out written words struggle to match letters to their proper sounds.
- **Fluency.** People who lack fluency have difficulty reading quickly, accurately, and with proper expression (if reading aloud).
- **Poor reading comprehension.** People with poor reading comprehension have trouble understanding what they read.

WHAT CAUSES READING DISORDERS?

Reading disorders involve specific, brain-based difficulties in learning to recognize and decipher printed words. There is no single known cause at this time. Environmental factors—such as children's experiences in the classroom or whether they were read to often as preschoolers—can play a significant role in reading ability. In addition, research suggests that difficulty with reading may be linked to a person's genes. This finding means that reading disorders can pass from one generation to the next. For example, some cases of reading disorders are associated with a change in genes that play a role in prenatal brain development.

WHAT ARE THE SYMPTOMS OF READING DISORDERS?

People with reading disorders often have different combinations of symptoms. Symptoms can include the following:
- problems sounding out words
- difficulty recognizing sounds and the letters that make up those sounds
- poor spelling
- slow reading
- problems reading out loud with the correct expression
- problems understanding what was just read

HOW ARE READING DISORDERS DIAGNOSED?

Providers usually use a series of tests to diagnose a reading disorder. They assess a person's memory, spelling abilities, visual perception, and reading skills. Family history, a child's history of response to instruction, and other assessments might also be involved. Although the *Eunice Kennedy Shriver* National Institute of Child Health and Human Development (NICHD) studies reading and reading disorders, the institute is not involved with setting definitions or guidelines for diagnosing reading disorders.

The U.S. Department of Education (ED) offers services and assistance for people with reading disorders through its Office of Special Education Programs (OSEP). The OSEP also supports the Center for Parent Information and Resources (CPIR), which can help parents learn about their children's reading or other learning disorders. The CPIR helps parents find professionals to assist with children's treatment and education. It also provides information about the laws and policies related to education for a child with a reading disorder or learning disability.

WHAT ARE COMMON TREATMENTS FOR READING DISORDERS?

The best treatment strategy for a reading disorder depends on the needs of the individual. In general, teachers with special training provide the most effective instruction. The instruction should be intensive. And, the earlier children receive help, the better the results. Reading disorders cannot be cured. But, with proper instruction, people with these disorders can overcome specific problems, learn to read, and improve fluency and comprehension. There is no single treatment for reading disorders.[1]

---

[1] "Reading and Reading Disorders," *Eunice Kennedy Shriver* National Institute of Child Health and Human Development (NICHD), March 5, 2020. Available online. URL: www.nichd.nih.gov/health/topics/reading. Accessed February 5, 2024.

Section 4.2 | Understanding Dyslexia

Dyslexia occurs in people of all backgrounds and intellectual levels. People with dyslexia can be very bright. They are often capable or even gifted in areas such as art, computer science, design, drama, electronics, math, mechanics, music, physics, sales, and sports. Some of America's most well-known and successful individuals have confronted the challenge of dyslexia.

WHAT IS DYSLEXIA?
Dyslexia specifically impairs a person's ability to read. Individuals typically read at significantly lower levels than expected despite having normal intelligence. Although it varies from person to person, people with dyslexia have difficulty with sound processing, spelling, and/or rapid visual-verbal responding. Adult onset of dyslexia usually results from brain injury or dementia; this contrasts with those with dyslexia who simply were never identified as children or adolescents. Dyslexia can be inherited in some families.

SYMPTOMS OF DYSLEXIA
People with dyslexia often show:
- difficulty and slowness in reading words
- difficulty understanding the text that is read (poor comprehension)
- problems with spelling
- delayed speech (learning to talk later than most other children)
- difficulty with rhyming

TREATING DYSLEXIA
The main focus of treatment should be on a person's specific learning problems, typically by modifying the teaching environment and methods.
- **Special teaching techniques**. These techniques use explicit, systematic instruction to teach and directly support children's efforts to learn to read and recognize words. This occurs over time.

- **Classroom modifications.** Teachers can give students with dyslexia extra time to finish tasks and provide taped tests that allow the child to hear the questions instead of reading them.
- **Use of technology.** Children with dyslexia may benefit from listening to books on tape or using word processing programs with spell-check features.

SPECIAL EDUCATION SERVICES

The Individuals with Disabilities Education Act (IDEA) requires public schools to provide free special education support to children with learning and other disabilities. They must be taught in the least restrictive and most appropriate environments for them.

In most states, children are entitled to these services beginning at the age of three and extending through high school or until the age of 21, whichever comes first. The teaching environment should be designed to meet the child's specific needs and skills. It should minimize restrictions on the child's access to typical learning experiences. The specific rules of the IDEA for each state are available from the National Early Childhood Technical Assistance Center (NECTAC).

Qualifying for Special Education

To qualify for special education services, a child must be evaluated by the school system and meet specific criteria outlined in federal and state guidelines. To learn how to have a child assessed for special services, parents and caregivers should contact a local school principal or special education coordinator. Parents can also visit the following web resources:
- the Parent Technical Assistance Center Network (www.parentcenternetwork.org)
- the Parent Guide to the IDEA (www.ncld.org/parents-child-disabilities/idea-guide)

WHAT RESEARCH IS BEING DONE?

The *Eunice Kennedy Shriver* National Institute of Child Health and Human Development (NICHD) and other institutes of the National Institutes of Health (NIH) support dyslexia research through grants to major research institutions across the country. Research avenues focus on developing techniques to diagnose and treat dyslexia and other learning disabilities, increasing the understanding of the biological and possible genetic bases of learning disabilities, and exploring treatments to improve outcomes for children and adults with dyslexia.

TALK WITH YOUR CHILD, READ TO YOUR CHILD EVERY DAY

Brett Miller, PhD, Program Director, Child Development and Behavior Branch (CDBB) of the NICHD, takes a few questions on dyslexia.

Is There a Key to Helping People with Dyslexia?

Early, systematic, and explicit reading instruction—teaching the connection between the written word and its specific sounds—is critical for dyslexia. The written word maps directly onto spoken language. So the challenge is to combine the sounds of English, for example, to the specific letters of the alphabet.

How Can Parents Help Their Children?

Since learning begins at home, the best thing parents can do is to talk with their children and read to them every day. Let them soak in what they are hearing and learn how to converse. This is a great opportunity to bond with your children and help them build their oral vocabulary and learn the structure of language, which is part of the foundation for reading.

What Is the Goal?

The goal is to build a foundation for reading, and that takes lots of time and practice.

When Should Special Instruction Begin?

The earlier, the better for children who are struggling to read. Some children need more time to learn, while others do better in smaller groups. So parents should build relationships with their children's teachers and school administrators to advocate for the best possible support. Early intervention reduces long-term problems. Children who are not improving by the fourth or fifth grade may need continued instructional support on foundational skills of reading in later grades.

WHAT IS THE PROGNOSIS?

For those with dyslexia, the prognosis is mixed. The disability affects such a wide range of people and produces such different symptomsand varying severity that predictions are hard to make. Prognosis is generally good, however, for individuals whose dyslexia is identified early, who have supportive family and friends and a strong self-image, and who are involved in proper remediation.[2]

---

[2] MedlinePlus, "NIH MedlinePlus the Magazine Winter 2016," National Institutes of Health (NIH), 2016. Available online. URL: https://magazine.medlineplus.gov/pdf/MLPWinter16.pdf. Accessed February 5, 2024.

Chapter 5 | Dysgraphia

Dysgraphia is a learning disorder characterized by incorrect spelling, poor handwriting, and trouble choosing the right word. It is a neurological disorder and can occur in children and adults. In children, the evidence of dysgraphia is seen when they are introduced to writing.

CAUSES OF DYSGRAPHIA

The causes of dysgraphia are unknown; however, in children, it is often associated with problems in orthographic coding (an ability to remember written words in working memory).

This learning disorder may be present in children along with other learning disabilities such as dyslexia and attention deficit hyperactivity disorder (ADHD). In adults, it may result from damage to the parietal lobe of the brain.

SYMPTOMS OF DYSGRAPHIA

Messy, irregular, or inconsistent writing is often associated with dysgraphia. But not all who have untidy handwriting have dysgraphia. Neat handwriting is possible with dysgraphia, although learning to write neatly may take a long time. The following are common characteristics of dysgraphia:
- slow writing
- incorrect spelling
- incorrect capitalization
- difficulty copying words
- a mix of uppercase and lowercase letters
- a mix of cursive and print letters
- different sized letters
- unfinished words

- an odd or tight grip on the pencil or pen
- inappropriate letter spacing
- poor use of lines
- reading out loud while writing
- unusual position of the hand, body, or paper while writing

TYPES OF DYSGRAPHIA

- **Dyslexic dysgraphia.** For a person with this form of dysgraphia, their written work that is not copied from a source is illegible. Copied work (writing or drawing) may be clear, although spelling skills are poor. Also, their finger-tapping speed (a method to identify fine motor problems) is normal. Despite the name, this form of dysgraphia may also be present without dyslexia.
- **Motor dysgraphia.** This form of dysgraphia is a result of poor fine motor skills. People with motor dysgraphia may also have poor dexterity. Even though copied from a source, their work is illegible and may have a slant due to poor grip on the pencil or pen. It takes extreme effort and a great deal of time to present a short, written assignment. They have below-average finger-tapping speed results, but their spelling skills are not impaired.
- **Spatial dysgraphia.** Those with spatial dysgraphia have trouble staying between the lines and spacing out the words due to a lack of spatial understanding. Their writing or drawing, both copied and spontaneous, is illegible, but spelling is not impaired, and finger-tapping speed is average.
- **Phonological dysgraphia.** This is characterized by difficulty processing (writing and spelling) nonwords, unfamiliar words, and phonetically irregular words. People with this type of dysgraphia have trouble remembering phonemes (distinct units of sound) and using them to form a target word.
- **Lexical dysgraphia.** This form of dysgraphia is very rare in children. It is characterized by misspelling irregular words as the person depends on the standard sound-to-letter pattern.

DIAGNOSIS OF DYSGRAPHIA

Diagnosis for dysgraphia is often made with a team of specialists that involves a pediatrician or family physician and a licensed psychologist. A pediatrician helps rule out other conditions that may cause writing problems. A psychologist uses written and academic tests, intelligence quotient (IQ) tests, and motor skills challenges. They observe the child's grip, posture, hand, and body movement, as well as the writing process, to make a diagnosis.

TREATMENT OF DYSGRAPHIA

There is no cure for dysgraphia, but symptoms can be managed with the help of occupational therapy. Treatment for dysgraphia differs from child to child and depends on other health conditions or learning disorders that the child may have. Children with ADHD and dysgraphia have shown some improvement in both conditions from ADHD medication. The following may help children with dysgraphia:
- Encourage their effort, and do not criticize shabby work.
- Try different writing aids to make writing easier.
- Use the connect-the-dots puzzle.
- Practice drawing lines within mazes.
- Use paper with raised lines to help teach letter alignment.
- Use a stress ball to improve hand-muscle coordination and strength.

References

Leonard, Janye. "What Is Dysgraphia?" Medical News Today, July 15, 2020. Available online. URL: www.medicalnewstoday.com/articles/dysgraphia. Accessed February 22, 2024.

Miller, Kelli. "What Is Dysgraphia? What Should I Do If My Child Has It?" WebMD, December 16, 2022. Available online. URL: www.webmd.com/add-adhd/childhood-adhd/dysgraphia-facts. Accessed February 22, 2024.

Roland, James. "What Is Dysgraphia?" Healthline, December 7, 2018. Available online. URL: www.healthline.com/health/what-is-dysgraphia. Accessed February 22, 2024.

Chapter 6 | Dyscalculia

WHAT IS DYSCALCULIA?
Dyscalculia is not as well-known as "dyslexia," but both are learning disabilities. Also called a "math learning disability," dyscalculia causes trouble with:
- understanding arithmetic (numbers) concepts and solving arithmetic problems
- estimating time, measuring, and budgeting

WHAT FACTORS INDICATE A CHILD MAY HAVE DYSCALCULIA?
- Children aged four may have trouble:
  - listing numbers in the correct order
  - matching number words or written digits to the number of objects
  - counting objects
- Children aged 6–12 may have regular and lasting trouble:
  - performing addition, subtraction, multiplication, or division appropriate to the grade level
  - recognizing math errors
- Children over the age of 12 may have trouble:
  - estimating (informed guessing)
  - making exact calculations
  - understanding graphs and charts
  - understanding fractions and decimals

HOW CAN ADULTS HELP CHILDREN WHO SHOW SIGNS OF DYSCALCULIA?
Show the child that numbers are a normal part of everyday life.
- Mention numbers to your child while doing everyday activities, such as grocery shopping or setting the table.

- Count out loud and show the child both the written number word ("three") and digit ("3").
- Count actual objects the child can see.
- Compare objects in everyday conversation using words that describe size or amount.[1]

SYMPTOMS OF DYSCALCULIA

In early childhood, dyscalculia is typified by general difficulty with numbers, recognizing patterns, and sorting objects by shape or size Symptoms include:
- lack of understanding of time needed for tasks
- miscalculating time taken for tasks
- difficulty applying math principles to everyday life
- poor sense of direction, easily gets lost, or worries about getting lost
- trouble judging distances between objects
- may do well in classes that require reading and writing skills but struggles in those that rely on numbers
- difficulty understanding information in chart or graph form
- good memory of spoken or printed words but has trouble remembering numbers and patterns

DIAGNOSIS OF DYSCALCULIA

Most often, various types of learning disabilities are identified when children are quite young. Younger students do so well in other areas, and the level of math being taught is simple enough that they are able to mask the symptoms of dyscalculia. As a result, in some cases, it may not be diagnosed until teenage, when working with numbers becomes considerably more complex.

There is no single cause for dyscalculia, but because some of the underlying problems can be neurological or genetic, the first step in diagnosis should be a physical examination by a doctor who is

---

[1] "Infographic: Does Your Child Struggle with Math? (Text Alternative)," *Eunice Kennedy Shriver National Institute of Child Health and Human Development* (NICHD), December 30, 2017. Available online. URL: www.nichd.nih.gov/newsroom/digital-media/infographics/MathLearningDisability-txtalt. Accessed February 5, 2024.

aware that the teen has been exhibiting symptoms. If no physical cause can be determined, then the student should be evaluated by a specialist in learning disabilities, who reviews past performance, administers a variety of tests, and asks questions to determine the individual's skills and understanding of various concepts. Some of the evaluation processes include:
- questions about areas in which the student feels they have had difficulty
- questions about times when the student has felt hopeless or frustrated about math
- probing for other learning disabilities that may be contributing factors
- an evaluation of basic math skills
- determining whether the student can distinguish patterns and organize objects logically
- evaluating the individual's ability to handle money
- assessing the student's ability to find ways to solve problems
- evaluating the ability to estimate time taken for tasks

An important part of diagnosis is to evaluate how well the individual is able to understand math concepts and apply them to common situations rather than just having them perform a series of calculations.

TREATMENT OF DYSCALCULIA

Dyscalculia cannot be cured, and it will not improve on its own. However, with treatment by a trained professional and support from teachers, parents, and peers, math skills can be considerably improved. Some strategies include the following:
- helping students be aware of their strengths and weaknesses so they can understand and make use of their own learning style
- associating math skills to everyday situations
- breaking complex problems into smaller parts
- using drawings or physical objects to help solve math problems

- working on a calculator if required
- circling computation signs before trying to solve a problem
- covering most of the math exercise or test with a piece of paper to make it easier to concentrate on one problem at a time
- playing math-related video games
- reading math problems aloud and continuing to talk while working on a solution
- reviewing new skills, discussing, and asking questions before moving on to the next task
- engaging a tutor to help with review, practice, and any particular areas of difficulty
- working with a classmate on homework assignments and reviewing the day's lessons

References

Morin, Amanda. "Treatment for Kids with Dyscalculia," Understood, October 31, 2017. Available online. URL: www.understood.org/en/learning-attention-issues/treatments-approaches/treatment-options/treatment-options-for-dyscalculia. Accessed February 21, 2024.

"What Is Dyscalculia?" Understood, September 24, 2014. Available online. URL: www.understood.org/en/learning-attention-issues/child-learning-disabilities/dyscalculia/understanding-dyscalculia. Accessed February 21, 2024.

"What Is Dyscalculia?" Dyslexia SPELD Foundation, May 21, 2015. Available online. URL: https://dsf.net.au/what-is-dyscalculia. Accessed February 21, 2024.

Chapter 7 | Learning Disability and Comorbid Conditions

Chapter Contents
Section 7.1—Language and Speech Disorders 46
Section 7.2—Specific Language Impairment 49
Section 7.3—Auditory Processing Disorder..............................52
Section 7.4—Visual Processing Disorders................................55
Section 7.5—Developmental Dyspraxia..................................59
Section 7.6—Nonverbal Learning Disability 62

Section 7.1 | Language and Speech Disorders

Children are born ready to learn a language, but they need to learn the language or languages that their family and environment use. Learning a language takes time, and children vary in how quickly they master milestones in language and speech development. Typically, developing children may have trouble with some sounds, words, and sentences while they are learning. However, most children can use language easily around five years of age.

HELPING CHILDREN LEARN LANGUAGE

Parents and caregivers are the most important teachers during a child's early years. Children learn language by listening to others speak and by practicing. Even young babies notice when others repeat and respond to the noises and sounds they make. Children's language and brain skills get stronger if they hear many different words. Parents can help their children learn in many different ways, such as:

- responding to the first sounds, gurgles, and gestures a baby makes
- repeating what the child says and adding to it
- talking about the things that a child sees
- asking questions and listening to the answers
- looking at or reading books
- telling stories
- singing songs and sharing rhymes

This can happen both during playtime and during daily routines. Parents can also observe the following:

- how their child hears and talks and compare it with typical milestones for communication skills
- how their child reacts to sounds and have their hearing tested if they have concerns

WHAT TO DO IF THERE ARE CONCERNS

Some children struggle with understanding and speaking, and they need help. They may not master the language milestones at the

Learning Disability and Comorbid Conditions | 47

same time as other children, and it may be a sign of a language or speech delay or disorder.

Language development has different parts, and children might have problems with one or more of the following:
- **Receptive language.** Understanding what others say. This could be due to:
  - not hearing the words (hearing loss)
  - not understanding the meaning of the words
- **Expressive language.** Communicating thoughts using language. This could be due to:
  - not knowing the words to use
  - not knowing how to put words together
  - knowing the words to use but not being able to express them

Language and speech disorders can exist together or by themselves. Examples of problems with language and speech development include the following:
- speech disorders:
  - difficulty with forming specific words or sounds correctly
  - difficulty with making words or sentences flow smoothly, such as stuttering or stammering
- language delay:
  - the ability to understand and speak developing more slowly than is typical
- language disorders:
  - aphasia (difficulty understanding or speaking parts of language due to a brain injury or how the brain works)
  - auditory processing disorder (APD; difficulty understanding the meaning of the sounds that the ear sends to the brain)

Language or speech disorders can occur with other learning disorders that affect reading and writing. Children with language disorders may feel frustrated that they cannot understand others or make themselves understood and they may act out, act helpless, or withdraw. Language or speech disorders can also be present with emotional or behavioral disorders, such as attention deficit hyperactivity disorder (ADHD) or anxiety. Children with developmental disabilities, including autism spectrum disorder (ASD), may also have difficulties with speech and language. The combination of challenges can make it particularly hard for a child to succeed in school. Properly diagnosing a child's disorder is crucial so that each child can get the right kind of help.

DETECTING PROBLEMS WITH LANGUAGE OR SPEECH

If a child has a problem with language or speech development, talk to a health-care provider about an evaluation. An important first step is to find out if the child may have hearing loss. Hearing loss may be difficult to notice, particularly if a child has hearing loss only in one ear or has partial hearing loss, which means they can hear some sounds but not others. A language development specialist, such as a speech-language pathologist, will conduct a careful assessment to determine what type of problem with language or speech the child may have.

Overall, learning more than one language does not cause language disorders, but children may not follow exactly the same developmental milestones as those who learn only one language. Developing the ability to understand and speak in two languages depends on how much practice the child has using both languages and the kind of practice. If a child who is learning more than one language has difficulty with language development, careful assessment by a specialist who understands the development of skills in more than one language may be needed.

TREATMENT FOR LANGUAGE OR SPEECH DISORDERS AND DELAYS

Children with language problems often need extra help and special instruction. Speech-language pathologists can work directly with children and their parents, caregivers, and teachers.

Having a language or speech delay or disorder can qualify a child for early intervention (for children up to three years of age) and special education services (for children aged three and older). Schools can do their own testing for language or speech disorders to see if a child needs intervention. An evaluation by a health-care

Learning Disability and Comorbid Conditions | 49

professional is needed if there are other concerns about the child's hearing, behavior, or emotions. Parents, health-care providers, and the school can work together to find the right referrals and treatment.[1]

Section 7.2 | Specific Language Impairment

WHAT IS SPECIFIC LANGUAGE IMPAIRMENT?

Specific language impairment (SLI) is a communication disorder that interferes with the development of language skills in children who have no hearing loss. SLI can affect a child's speaking, listening, reading, and writing. SLI is also called "developmental language disorder" (DLD), language delay, or developmental dysphasia. It is one of the most common developmental disorders, affecting approximately 7–10 percent of children in kindergarten. Of those children with language impairment, approximately 2–3 percent also have an existing medical condition and/or intellectual disability. The effect of SLI usually persists into adulthood.

WHAT CAUSES SPECIFIC LANGUAGE IMPAIRMENT?

The cause of SLI is unknown, but discoveries suggest that it has a strong genetic link. Children with SLI are more likely than those without SLI to have parents and siblings who have also had difficulties and delays in speaking. In fact, 50–70 percent of children with SLI have at least one family member with the disorder. Learning more than one language at a time does not cause SLI. The disorder can, however, affect both multilingual children and children who speak only one language.

---

[1] National Center on Birth Defects and Developmental Disabilities (NCBDDD), "Language and Speech Disorders in Children," Centers for Disease Control and Prevention (CDC), May 11, 2022. Available online. URL: www.cdc.gov/ncbddd/developmentaldisabilities/language-disorders.html. Accessed February 6, 2024.

WHAT ARE THE SYMPTOMS OF SPECIFIC LANGUAGE IMPAIRMENT?

A child with SLI often has a history of being a late talker (reaching spoken language milestones later than peers). Preschool-aged children with SLI may:
- be late to put words together into sentences
- struggle to learn new words and make conversation
- have difficulty following directions, not because they are stubborn but because they do not fully understand the words spoken to them
- make frequent grammatical errors when speaking

Although some late talkers eventually catch up with peers, children with SLI have persistent language difficulties. Symptoms common in older children and adults with SLI include the following:
- limited use of complex sentences
- difficulty finding the right words
- difficulty understanding figurative language
- reading problems
- disorganized storytelling and writing
- frequent grammatical and spelling errors

HOW IS SPECIFIC LANGUAGE IMPAIRMENT DIAGNOSED?

If a doctor, teacher, or parent suspects that a child has SLI, a speech-language pathologist (a professional trained to assess and treat people with speech or language problems) can evaluate the child's language skills. The type of evaluation depends on the child's age and the concerns that led to the evaluation. In general, an evaluation includes the following:
- direct observation of the child
- interviews and questionnaires completed by parents and/or teachers
- assessments of the child's learning ability
- standardized tests of current language performance

These tools allow the speech-language pathologist to compare the child's language skills to those of same-age peers, identify specific difficulties, and plan for potential treatment targets.

IS SPECIFIC LANGUAGE IMPAIRMENT THE SAME THING AS A LEARNING DISABILITY?

Specific language impairment is not the same thing as a learning disability. Instead, SLI is a risk factor for learning disabilities since problems with basic language skills affect classroom performance. This means that children with SLI are more likely to be diagnosed with a learning disability than children who do not have SLI. They may struggle with translating letters into sounds for reading. Their writing skills may be weakened by grammatical errors, limited vocabulary, and problems with comprehension and organizing thoughts into coherent sentences. Difficulties with language comprehension can make mathematical word problems challenging. Some children with SLI may show signs of dyslexia. By the time they reach adulthood, people with SLI are six times more likely to be diagnosed with reading and spelling disabilities and four times more likely to be diagnosed with math disabilities than those who do not have SLI.

IS SPECIFIC LANGUAGE IMPAIRMENT A LIFELONG CONDITION?

Specific language impairment is a developmental disorder, which means that its symptoms first appear in childhood. This does not mean that as children develop, they grow out of the problem. Instead, the problem is apparent in early childhood and will likely continue but change with development. For instance, a young child with SLI might use ungrammatical sentences in conversation, while a young adult with SLI might avoid complex sentences in conversations and struggle to produce clear, concise, well-organized, and grammatically accurate writing. Early treatment during the preschool years can improve the skills of many children with language delays, including those with SLI. Children who enter kindergarten with significant language delays are likely to continue having problems, but they and even older children can still benefit from treatment. Many adults develop strategies for managing SLI symptoms. This can improve their daily social, family, and work lives.

WHAT ARE THE TREATMENTS AVAILABLE FOR SPECIFIC LANGUAGE IMPAIRMENT?

Treatment services for SLI are typically provided or overseen by a licensed speech-language pathologist. Treatment may be provided

in homes, schools, university programs for speech-language pathology, private clinics, or outpatient hospital settings. Identifying and treating children with SLI early in life is ideal, but people can respond well to treatment regardless of when it begins. Treatment depends on the age and needs of the person. Starting treatment early can help young children:
- acquire missing elements of grammar
- expand their understanding and use of words
- develop social communication skills

For school-age children, treatment may focus on understanding instruction in the classroom, including helping with issues such as:
- following directions
- understanding the meaning of the words that teachers use
- organizing information
- improving speaking, reading, and writing skills

Adults entering new jobs, vocational programs, or higher education may need help learning technical vocabulary or improving workplace writing skills.[2]

Section 7.3 | Auditory Processing Disorder

WHAT IS AUDITORY PROCESSING DISORDER?
Auditory processing disorder (APD), or central auditory processing disorder, is a hearing disorder caused by a lack of coordination between the ear and brain. Sound waves that travel into the ear are converted into vibrations in the middle ear. After reaching the inner ear, these vibrations are converted to electrical signals, and then, with the help of the auditory nerves, they reach the brain. The brain then analyzes the signals and turns them into a sound that can be recognized. Interference in this step prevents individuals from "hearing" sounds the usual way.

[2] "Specific Language Impairment," National Institute on Deafness and Other Communication Disorders (NIDCD), July 15, 2019. Available online. URL: www.nidcd.nih.gov/sites/default/files/Documents/health/voice/specific-language-impairment.pdf. Accessed February 6, 2024.

Learning Disability and Comorbid Conditions | 53

Signs of APD generally begin in childhood, although it can occur at all ages. APD can occur along with conditions such as attention deficit hyperactivity disorder (ADHD) and autism spectrum disorder (ASD) but is not a result of these conditions.

CAUSES OF AUDITORY PROCESSING DISORDER
The exact causes of APD are not known. However, some potential risk factors include:
- genetics
- chronic ear infections
- meningitis
- head injury
- premature birth or low birth weight
- lead poisoning
- multiple sclerosis (MS)
- developmental delay
- neurological changes due to aging

SYMPTOMS OF AUDITORY PROCESSING DISORDER
The following symptoms can vary from mild to severe:
- difficulty following and responding to conversations
- difficulty recognizing where the sound is coming from
- easily distracted or bothered by sudden or loud noise
- difficulty paying attention
- difficulty remembering verbal instructions
- difficulty distinguishing between similar sounds
- experiencing difficulty in reading, writing, and speaking

DIAGNOSIS OF AUDITORY PROCESSING DISORDER
A multidisciplinary team, including teachers, a physician, a psychologist, a speech-language therapist, and an audiologist, is involved in diagnosing APD due to the complex nature of the auditory process. A physician can rule out potential causes of APD. Teachers can shed light on learning challenges, a psychologist can identify cognitive functions, and a speech-language therapist can evaluate written and oral communication skills. Along with the multidisciplinary team's information, an audiologist conducts a series of advanced

listening tests to make a diagnosis. The audiologist looks for issues in the following areas:
- **Auditory memory problems.** Difficulty remembering information such as instructions, directions, or lists.
- **Auditory attention problems.** Difficulty paying attention long enough to receive instructions.
- **Auditory discrimination problems.** Experiencing trouble distinguishing between words with similar sounds
- **Auditory figure-ground problems.** Inability to pay attention in noisy situations.
- **Auditory cohesion problems.** Tasks requiring high-level listening are difficult (e.g., understanding verbal math problems or riddles).

Children are not usually tested for APD until they are six to seven years of age because kids who are younger than this age group may not give accurate responses for their listening tests. An audiologist uses assessment tests that help evaluate the following:
- ability to recognize a pattern in sounds
- whether the condition is due to APD or hearing loss
- brain activity while listening to sounds on a headphone
- ability to understand speech in various scenarios (rapid speech, noisy environment)
- ability to pick up changes in pitch

TREATMENT OF AUDITORY PROCESSING DISORDER

There is no cure for APD, and treatment varies from person to person. The treatment focuses on the following three primary areas:
- **Auditory training (therapy).** This kind of training can be done with a therapist, either online or one-on-one. It aims to improve a person's ability to identify sound patterns, where the sound is coming from, and focus on specific sounds amidst background noise.
- **Changing the learning or working environment.** The following measures can help those with APD:
  - using assistive technology such as frequency modulators (FMs)

- avoiding things such as fans, radios, and televisions that generate background noise
- requesting teachers to use visual aids in class along with lectures
- sitting in the front row of the class to focus on what is being taught
• **Compensatory strategies.** These focus on strengthening cognitive skills such as attention and memory, problem-solving, and language.

References

"Auditory Processing Disorder," KidsHealth, February 8, 2021. Available online. URL: https://kidshealth.org/en/parents/central-auditory.html. Accessed February 6, 2024.

"Understanding Auditory Processing Disorder in Children," American Speech-Language-Hearing Association (ASHA), April 4, 2014. Available online. URL: www.asha.org/public/hearing/understanding-auditory-processing-disorders-in-children. Accessed February 6, 2024.

"What Is Auditory Processing Disorder?" WebMD, May 12, 2023. Available online. URL: www.webmd.com/brain/auditory-processing-disorder#1. Accessed February 6, 2024.

"What Is Auditory Processing Disorder (APD)?" Healthline, January 27, 2020. Available online. URL: www.healthline.com/health/auditory-processing-disorder#takeaway. Accessed February 6, 2024.

Section 7.4 | Visual Processing Disorders

WHAT ARE VISUAL PROCESSING DISORDERS?

Visual processing disorders are weaknesses in the brain functions that process visual input. Although the eyes are the organs that receive visual images in the form of light, the brain must process these images and interpret them. People with visual processing issues may have good eyesight, but their brains do not accurately receive or interpret the visual signals from their eyes. These weaknesses can create challenges in many areas of life, from recognizing letters and symbols, to distinguishing objects in space, to remembering things that have been seen.

Although visual processing issues are common in children with learning disabilities—and especially those with dyslexia—they are not considered learning disabilities by themselves. Nevertheless, they may affect many areas of learning, such as reading, writing, vocabulary, verbal expression, memory, and attention. In addition to affecting learning, visual processing issues can affect socialization and self-esteem. While medical research has not uncovered the cause of visual processing issues, evidence suggests that preterm birth, low birth weight, and traumatic brain injury (TBI) may increase the likelihood of visual processing issues.

SYMPTOMS OF VISUAL PROCESSING DISORDERS

Visual processing issues can be difficult to recognize, but there are some relatively common symptoms in children, including:
- being clumsy or bumping into things
- experiencing difficulty writing or coloring within the lines
- reversing or misreading letters, words, and numbers
- difficulty remembering sequences or numbers or spelling of words
- trouble paying attention to visual tasks or being distracted by visual information
- showing a lack of interest in movies, television, or video presentations
- having trouble with reading comprehension or remembering information when reading silently (especially when combined with strong verbal skills and oral comprehension)
- having trouble copying notes or recognizing changes in classroom displays, signs, or notices
- having weak math skills, confusing mathematical signs and symbols, or omitting steps in equations
- frequently rubbing the eyes or complaining about eye strain

Learning Disability and Comorbid Conditions | 57

DIAGNOSIS OF VISUAL PROCESSING DISORDERS

Diagnosing a visual processing disorder involves several steps. The first step is to take notes and keep records of the problems experienced by the child. The next step involves taking the child to a pediatrician or pediatric optometrist to conduct a basic vision test and look for health issues involving the eyes. If there are no significant problems with the child's eye health, the next step is to obtain a reference to a neuropsychologist.

Neuropsychologists are trained to diagnose visual processing issues and can perform tests to determine the extent to which these weaknesses may be affecting the child's development. Researchers have identified eight different types of visual processing disorders, each of which affects different skills and creates its own challenges. The types of visual processing issues include the following:

- **Visual discrimination.** People with this type of issue have trouble comparing similar items—such as letters, shapes, patterns, or objects—and telling the difference between them. They may mix up letters such as d and b, or h and n.
- **Visual sequencing.** People with this type of visual processing issue have difficulty distinguishing the order of letters, numbers, words, symbols, or images.
- **Visual figure-ground discrimination.** This type of issue is characterized by difficulty seeing a shape or image against a background. People with this issue may not be able to locate a certain piece of information on a page or screen.
- **Visual memory.** People with this type of issue have difficulty remembering what they have seen or read, whether recently (short term) or some time ago (long term).
- **Visual-spatial relationships.** Individuals with this type of issue have trouble seeing where objects are positioned in space. They may experience challenges in understanding distances, reading maps, judging time, or picturing the relationship of objects described in writing or in a spoken narrative.
- **Visual closure.** People with this type of issue have trouble recognizing familiar objects if a part of the object is missing. They may not be able to identify a face if the mouth

is missing in a picture, or if a letter is missing in a familiar word.
- **Letter and symbol reversal.** People with this issue tend to reverse letters or numbers when reading or writing. They may also struggle with letter formation.
- **Visual-motor processing.** People with this issue have difficulty coordinating bodily movements using feedback from the eyes. They may appear uncoordinated or clumsy and bump into things.

TREATMENT OF VISUAL PROCESSING DISORDERS

Although there is no cure for visual processing disorders, there are many different strategies that can help people improve their skills and adapt to the challenges they face. Teachers and paraprofessionals at school may offer valuable assistance for children who are diagnosed with visual processing issues. Some of these children may qualify for special education services and receive an Individualized Education Program (IEP), which outlines the specific support the school must provide. Schools may also provide informal support to meet the children's needs, such as allowing them to use books with large print or have tests read aloud.

Parents and caregivers can also help children with visual processing disorders improve their skills. Experts recommend writing out schedules and instructions in large print, with each step numbered clearly, and color-coding important points. It is also important to provide plenty of opportunities for children to practice visual processing skills through fun activities. Playing with jigsaw puzzles and estimating distances using a tape measure are examples of activities that improve visual processing skills.

References

Arky, Beth. "Understanding Visual Processing Issues," Understood, April 9, 2018. Available online. URL: www.deaf-ld.com/uploads/5/4/2/6/5426987/visual_processing_issues_%7C_visual_memory_problems_in_children.pdf. Accessed February 21, 2024.

Morin, Amanda. "Classroom Accommodations for Visual Processing Issues," Understood, April 1, 2015. Available online. URL: www.understood.org/en/articles/at-a-glance-classroom-accommodations-for-visual-processing-issues. Accessed February 21, 2024.

"Visual Processing Disorders: In Detail," LD Online, 2015. Available online. URL: www.ldonline.org/article/Visual_Processing_Disorders%3A_In_Detail?theme=print. Accessed February 21, 2024.

Section 7.5 | Developmental Dyspraxia

WHAT IS DYSPRAXIA?

The definitions for dyspraxia are varied and numerous, as are the names used to describe the disorder. The National Institute of Neurological Disorders and Stroke (NINDS) defines developmental dyspraxia as a disorder characterized by an impairment in the ability to plan and carry out sensory and motor tasks. Furthermore, all the definitions agree on what dyspraxia is not. It is not a muscle disorder although it involves muscle coordination and strength. It is not a cognitive disorder although it affects the ability to read, spell, and use language. It is a neurological disorder that involves motor planning in all areas of the body when the messages from the brain are unable to communicate directions to the muscles. Dyspraxia may be present in people with autism spectrum disorder (ASD), Asperger syndrome, and dyslexia. Stroke or other trauma may cause dyspraxia (acquired dyspraxia), or it may be present from birth (developmental dyspraxia).[3]

---

[3] "Giving a Face to a Hidden Disorder: The Impact of Dyspraxia," U.S. Department of Education (ED), September 2007. Available online. URL: https://files.eric.ed.gov/fulltext/EJ967468.pdf. Accessed February 6, 2024.

WHAT IS DEVELOPMENTAL DYSPRAXIA?

Developmental dyspraxia is a disorder characterized by an impairment in the ability to plan and carry out sensory and motor tasks. Generally, individuals with the disorder appear "out of sync" with their environment.[4]

WHO IS AFFECTED?

Dyspraxia is a largely unknown condition. It affects a significant number of both children and adults. Barbara Lantin, retired freelance health journalist, reports, "dyspraxia affects up to 10 percent (of the general population), 2 percent severely. As with dyslexia, 80 percent of those affected are boys." If daddy is clumsy or stumbles over speech, watch his sons carefully. Lawrence D. Shriberg, PhD, professor emeritus of Communicative Sciences and Disorders, University of Wisconsin, Madison, suggests, "Familial involvement is suspected due to the data collected on the occurrence in DAS families. Boys are overwhelmingly affected more than girls. The statistics range from a 3:1 ratio to as high as 9:1."

IDENTIFYING DYSPRAXIA

Dyspraxia is truly a hidden disorder. Parents who are certain that something is wrong with their child receive virtually no support from the medical and educational communities and are frequently misled by the word "yet." Typical responses to parental observations of problems with their child include, "He's just a late bloomer… he's just not crawling/walking/talking yet… I wouldn't worry about him yet." The word "yet" implies that waiting is an appropriate action and whatever the developmental milestone involved will simply come in time, both deleterious assumptions when dealing with dyspraxia since early intervention is crucial for children struggling with the developmental and academic issues presented by this disorder. B. Jacqueline Stordy, PhD, senior lecturer of Nutrition in the School of Biological Sciences at the

---

[4] "Developmental Dyspraxia," National Institute of Neurological Disorders and Stroke (NINDS), November 28, 2023. Available online. URL: www.ninds.nih.gov/health-information/disorders/developmental-dyspraxia. Accessed February 6, 2024.

University of Surrey, and Malcolm J. Nicholl, journalist on nutrition and education, reported, "A 1994 survey of 450 members of the Dyspraxia Foundation reported that most parents said they were aware that their child had a problem by age three but, on average, the official diagnosis was not made until the child was six and a half. Only a quarter of dyspraxic children are recognized as having the problem when they start school, and four out of five schools think the child will grow out of it." Often, pediatricians have little experience with dyspraxia and may simply assure worried moms that their son is just a little behind developmentally. "Many doctors have not yet become fully educated about dyspraxia and are just not aware that it is an acknowledged medical condition." Concerned parents fare no better when asking schools why their child is having difficulty, since the same 1994 survey revealed, astonishingly, that half of the children's teachers had never even heard of the condition of dyspraxia.

CAUSES OF DYSPRAXIA

There are a multitude of theories as to the cause of dyspraxia, but the answer remains a mystery. Most would contend that it is a neurological disorder although this is not documented. Various evaluations have shown these children to have no brain lesions or consistent differences in brain structure. The prevalent theory is that there is subtle brain impairment or malfunctioning. This impairment may be so slight or so specific that it is impossible to isolate or determine the cause. Birth or prenatal injuries or oxygen deprivation may have occurred in some cases; however, the majority of these children have no remarkable birth history. The bottom line is no one knows the specific cause.[5]

SYMPTOMS OF DEVELOPMENTAL DYSPRAXIA

Symptoms vary and may include the following:
- poor balance and coordination
- clumsiness
- vision problems

---

[5] See footnote [3].

- perception difficulties
- emotional and behavioral problems
- difficulty with reading, writing, and speaking
- poor social skills
- poor posture
- poor short-term memory

Although individuals with the disorder may be of average or above-average intelligence, they may behave immaturely.

TREATMENT OF DEVELOPMENTAL DYSPRAXIA

Treatment is symptomatic and supportive and may include occupational and speech therapy, "cueing," or other forms of communication, such as using pictures and hand gestures. Many children with the disorder require special education.

PROGNOSIS OF DEVELOPMENTAL DYSPRAXIA

Developmental dyspraxia is a lifelong disorder. Many individuals are able to compensate for their disabilities through occupational and speech therapy.[6]

Section 7.6 | Nonverbal Learning Disability

Nonverbal learning disability (NVLD) is a brain-based learning disability where individuals have difficulty with abstract thinking, spatial relationships, and identifying and interpreting concepts and patterns. It occurs in 0.1–1 percent of the general population and is also referred to as a "nonverbal learning disorder" or a right-hemisphere learning disorder.

Communication involves various forms, including spoken words. Sometimes individuals express exactly what they mean. On other occasions, they expect the listener to pick up another meaning from their facial expression or tone of voice. Sometimes

---

[6] See footnote [4].

they expect the listener to fill in information from past experience or some other source of information. For instance, "I love rainy days" is the truth when said directly. But, if the same phrase is said with a frown, eye roll, and a growly tone, the speaker is being sarcastic and is really telling the listener that the speaker dislikes rainy days. Finally, if the speaker says, "You know how I feel about rainy days," the listener is expected to fill in some previously learned information. A person with a NVLD cannot interpret the facial expressions and tone of voice of the sarcasm and thus takes the untrue statement as true. Nor can the listener draw on a pattern of previously learned information and thus truly not know how the speaker feels.

SIGNS OF NONVERBAL LEARNING DISABILITY

Children with NVLD tend to be very smart. They talk freely, develop large vocabularies in comparison to other children their age, memorize facts, and read early. Intelligence tests show high verbal intelligence quotient (IQ) but low performance IQ due to visual-spatial difficulties.

There are five main areas of weakness in people with NVLD. People with NVLD may not exhibit weakness in all five areas, nor may they exhibit them all at once. The weaknesses tend to become more obvious as children progress in school and are required to rely more on identifying patterns and less on memorized facts. The five main areas of weakness have been identified as follows:

- **Visual/spatial awareness.** Children with NVLD may have problems estimating the distance, size, and/or shape of objects. They may be clumsy, spill drinks, bump into people or objects, or not be able to catch a ball. They may also have a poor sense of direction, such as being able to distinguish left from right.
- **Motor skills.** Children with NVLD may have trouble mastering basic motor skills, both large (such as dressing themselves, running, or riding a bike) or small (such as writing or using scissors).
- **Abstract thinking.** Children with NVLD may have difficulty seeing or understanding the big picture. They

can read a story and relate the details but cannot answer questions about how the details fit together.
- **Conceptual skills.** Children with NVLD may have trouble grasping the larger concept of a situation (e.g., determining how pieces of a puzzle fit together to make a whole or identifying the steps needed to solve a problem). This contributes to problems, especially with math.
- **Social skills.** Children with NVLD may have trouble making friends or socializing in a group. They may interrupt or behave inappropriately in social situations. They use previously learned skills to cope with new social situations, whether appropriate or not.

In addition, because NVLD occurs in the right side of the brain, children with NVLD may have a distorted sense of touch or feel and poor coordination on the left side of the body. These areas of weakness are often masked in preschool and the early elementary grades when students are learning basic skills such as reading and arithmetic. By the fourth or fifth grade, when students are required to process what they read or remember patterns from previous examples, the weaknesses start to become evident. At the same time, these very smart children may start exhibiting behavioral problems brought on by frustration in not "getting it" or feelings of being a social reject.

DIAGNOSIS OF NONVERBAL LEARNING DISABILITY

The diagnosis of NVLD is controversial. NVLD is not listed in the *Diagnostic and Statistical Manual of Mental Disorders, Fifth Edition* (*DSM-5*) of the American Psychiatric Association, the manual used by doctors and therapists to diagnose learning disabilities. Nor is NVLD recognized as a disability covered by the Individuals with Disabilities Education Act (IDEA). Nonetheless, if a child is exhibiting signs of NVLD, there are steps parents should take to identify the problem.
- **Medical examination.** A thorough physical examination and a discussion of the child's learning problems will help the doctor rule out any physical causes for the learning problems.

- **Consulting mental health professionals.** Most likely, the family doctor will refer the child to a neurologist or other specialist. The specialist will talk to the parents and child about what is happening and may administer a variety of tests in the areas of speech and language, motor skills, and visual-spatial relationships. The results, coupled with information from the parents and child, will help the specialist analyze the strengths and weaknesses associated with NVLD and make a diagnosis.

As with many learning disorders, the symptoms of NVLD vary from child to child; thus, a comprehensive assessment is needed to determine the individual child's needs. With the input and support of learning professionals and therapists, as well as the family, steps can be taken to help the student with NVLD.

HELP FOR THOSE WITH NONVERBAL LEARNING DISABILITY

It is important to work with the child's school specialists to develop accommodations for the child's NVLD. Formal accommodation may be developed through an Individualized Education Program (IEP) or 504 plan. If the child does not qualify for either plan, informal accommodation may be made in the classroom. Classroom accommodations may include modifying homework assignments and tests for time and content, presenting lectures with PowerPoint slides, so the student can see as well as hear the material being covered, and/or working with a reading specialist to read a passage aloud and then extract key terms and ideas. Parents can help their children in various ways to make things easier for both the student and the family. They can:

- establish structure and routine
- give clear instructions
- keep a chart of the day's activities, both social and academic
- make transitions easier by giving logical, step-by-step explanations of what is going to happen
- break down tasks into small steps in a logical sequence

- play games with the child to have him or her identify emotions from facial expressions or voice tone
- avoid sarcasm or, if it happens, use the experience to help the child identify the signs of sarcasm
- set up one-on-one playdates with another child who shares an interest with yours (Playdates should be structured, monitored, and time-bound.)
- avoid situations that may overwhelm the child with too much sensory input (noise, smell, and activity)

There are other sources of help for parents and students. Social skills groups help the student in social situations, while parent behavioral training helps parents in learning how to collaborate with teachers. Occupational and physical therapy may help the child improve movement and writing skills as well as build tolerance for outside experiences. Cognitive therapy can help the child deal with anxiety, depression, and other mental health issues.

Although NVLD presents many challenges for both the student and the family, there is help available, and with patience and effort, there will be improvement.

References

Belsky, Gail. "What are Nonverbal Learning Disabilities?" Understood, June 24, 2021. Available online. URL: www.understood.org/en/articles/understanding-nonverbal-learning-disabilities. Accessed February 22, 2024.

Miller, Caroline. "What Is Nonverbal Learning Disorder?" Child Mind Institute, January 8, 2024. Available online. URL: https://childmind.org/article/what-is-non-verbal-learning-disorder. Accessed February 22, 2024.

"Quick Facts on Nonverbal Learning Disorder," Child Mind Institute, November 7, 2023. Available Online. URL: https://childmind.org/article/quick-facts-on-non-verbal-learning-disorder-nld. Accessed February 22, 2024.

Part 3 | Common Developmental Disorders That Affect Learning

Chapter 8 | Attention Deficit Hyperactivity Disorder

WHAT IS ATTENTION DEFICIT HYPERACTIVITY DISORDER?
Attention deficit hyperactivity disorder (ADHD) is one of the most common neurodevelopmental disorders of childhood. It is usually first diagnosed in childhood and often lasts into adulthood. Children with ADHD may have trouble paying attention, controlling impulsive behaviors (may act without thinking about what the result will be), or being overly active.

TYPES OF ATTENTION DEFICIT HYPERACTIVITY DISORDER
There are three different ways ADHD presents itself, depending on which types of symptoms are strongest in the individual:
- **Predominantly inattentive presentation.** It is hard for the individual to organize or finish a task, to pay attention to details, or to follow instructions or conversations. The person is easily distracted or forgets details of daily routines.
- **Predominantly hyperactive-impulsive presentation.** The person fidgets and talks a lot. It is hard to sit still for long (e.g., for a meal or while doing homework). Smaller children may run, jump, or climb constantly. The individual feels restless and has trouble with impulsivity. Someone who is impulsive may interrupt others a lot, grab things from people, or speak at inappropriate times. It is hard for the person to wait their turn or listen to directions. A person with impulsiveness may have more accidents and injuries than others.
- **Combined presentation.** Symptoms of the previously mentioned two types are equally present in the person.

Because symptoms can change over time, the presentation may change over time as well.

CAUSES OF ATTENTION DEFICIT HYPERACTIVITY DISORDER
Scientists are studying cause(s) and risk factors in an effort to find better ways to manage and reduce the chances of a person having ADHD. The cause(s) and risk factors for ADHD are unknown, but research shows that genetics plays an important role. In addition to genetics, scientists are studying other possible causes and risk factors, including the following:
- brain injury
- exposure to environmental risks (e.g., lead) during pregnancy or at a young age
- alcohol and tobacco use during pregnancy
- premature delivery
- low birth weight

Research does not support the popularly held views that ADHD is caused by eating too much sugar, watching too much television, parenting, or social and environmental factors, such as poverty or family chaos. Of course, many things, including these, might make symptoms worse, especially in certain people. But the evidence is not strong enough to conclude that they are the main causes of ADHD.

SIGNS AND SYMPTOMS OF ATTENTION DEFICIT HYPERACTIVITY DISORDER
It is normal for children to have trouble focusing and behaving at one time or another. However, children with ADHD do not just grow out of these behaviors. The symptoms continue, can be severe, and can cause difficulty at school, at home, or with friends. A child with ADHD might:
- daydream a lot
- forget or lose things a lot
- squirm or fidget
- talk too much

Attention Deficit Hyperactivity Disorder | 71

- make careless mistakes or take unnecessary risks
- have a hard time resisting temptation
- have trouble taking turns
- have difficulty getting along with others

DIAGNOSIS OF ATTENTION DEFICIT HYPERACTIVITY DISORDER

Deciding if a child has ADHD is a process with several steps. There is no single test to diagnose ADHD, and many other problems, such as anxiety, depression, sleep problems, and certain types of learning disabilities, can have similar symptoms. One step of the process involves having a medical exam, including hearing and vision tests, to rule out other problems with symptoms such as ADHD. Diagnosing ADHD usually includes a checklist for rating ADHD symptoms and taking a history of the child from parents, teachers, and sometimes the child.

TREATMENTS OF ATTENTION DEFICIT HYPERACTIVITY DISORDER

In most cases, ADHD is best treated with a combination of behavior therapy and medication. For preschool-aged children (4–5 years of age) with ADHD, behavior therapy, particularly training for parents, is recommended as the first line of treatment before medication is tried. What works best can depend on the child and family. Good treatment plans will include close monitoring, follow-ups, and making changes, if needed, along the way.

MANAGING SYMPTOMS: STAYING HEALTHY

Being healthy is important for all children and can be especially important for children with ADHD. In addition to behavioral therapy and medication, having a healthy lifestyle can make it easier for your child to deal with ADHD symptoms. Here are some healthy behaviors that may help:
- developing healthy eating habits, such as eating plenty of fruits, vegetables, and whole grains and choosing lean protein sources
- participating in daily physical activity based on age

- limiting the amount of daily screen time from televisions, computers, phones, and other electronics
- getting the recommended amount of sleep each night based on age[1]

---

[1] National Center on Birth Defects and Developmental Disabilities (NCBDDD), "What Is ADHD?" Centers for Disease Control and Prevention (CDC), September 27, 2023. Available online. URL: www.cdc.gov/ncbddd/adhd/facts.html. Accessed February 10, 2024.

Chapter 9 | Autism Spectrum Disorder

WHAT IS AUTISM SPECTRUM DISORDER?

Autism spectrum disorder (ASD) is a developmental disability caused by differences in the brain. Some people with ASD have a known difference, such as a genetic condition. Other causes are not yet known. Scientists believe there are multiple causes of ASD that act together to change the most common ways people develop.

People with ASD may behave, communicate, interact, and learn in ways that are different from most other people. There is often nothing about how they look that sets them apart from other people. The abilities of people with ASD can vary significantly. For example, some people with ASD may have advanced conversation skills, whereas others may be nonverbal. Some people with ASD need a lot of help in their daily lives; others can work and live with little to no support.

ASD begins before the age of three and can last throughout a person's life although symptoms may improve over time. Some children show ASD symptoms within the first 12 months of life. In others, symptoms may not show up until 24 months of age or later. Some children with ASD gain new skills and meet developmental milestones until around 18–24 months of age, and then they stop gaining new skills or lose the skills they once had.

As children with ASD become adolescents and young adults, they may have difficulties developing and maintaining friendships, communicating with peers and adults, or understanding what behaviors are expected in school or on the job. They may come to the attention of health-care providers because they also have conditions such as anxiety, depression, or attention deficit hyperactivity disorder (ADHD), which occur more often in people with ASD than in people without ASD.[1]

CAUSES AND RELATED FACTORS OF AUTISM SPECTRUM DISORDER

Researchers do not know the primary causes of ASD, but studies suggest that a person's genes can act together with aspects of their environment to affect development in ways that lead to ASD. Some factors that are associated with an increased likelihood of developing ASD include the following:

- having a sibling with ASD
- having older parents
- having certain genetic conditions (such as Down syndrome or fragile X syndrome (FXS))
- having a very low birth weight

SIGNS AND SYMPTOMS OF AUTISM SPECTRUM DISORDER

The following list gives some examples of common types of behaviors in people diagnosed with ASD. Not all people with ASD will have all behaviors, but most will have several of the behaviors listed subsequently.

Social communication/interaction behaviors may include the following:

- making little or inconsistent eye contact
- appearing not to look at or listen to people who are talking
- infrequently sharing interest, emotion, or enjoyment of objects or activities (including infrequent pointing at or showing things to others)
- not responding or being slow to respond to one's name or to other verbal bids for attention
- having difficulties with the back and forth of conversation
- often talking at length about a favorite subject without noticing that others are not interested or without giving others a chance to respond

---

[1] National Center on Birth Defects and Developmental Disabilities (NCBDDD), "What Is Autism Spectrum Disorder?" Centers for Disease Control and Prevention (CDC), December 9, 2022. Available online. URL: www.cdc.gov/ncbddd/autism/facts.html. Accessed February 6, 2024.

- displaying facial expressions, movements, and gestures that do not match what is being said
- having an unusual tone of voice that may sound singsong or flat and robot-like
- having trouble understanding another person's point of view or being unable to predict or understand other people's actions
- having difficulties adjusting behaviors to social situations
- having difficulties sharing in imaginative play or in making friends

Restrictive/repetitive behaviors may include the following:
- repeating certain behaviors or having unusual behaviors, such as repeating words or phrases (a behavior called "echolalia")
- having a lasting intense interest in specific topics, such as numbers, details, or facts
- showing overly focused interests, such as with moving objects or parts of objects
- becoming upset by slight changes in a routine and having difficulty with transitions
- being more sensitive or less sensitive than other people to sensory input, such as light, sound, clothing, or temperature

People with ASD may also experience sleep problems and irritability. People on the autism spectrum may also have many strengths, including the following:
- being able to learn things in detail and remember information for long periods of time
- being strong visual and auditory learners
- excelling in math, science, music, or art

DIAGNOSIS OF AUTISM SPECTRUM DISORDER
Health-care providers diagnose ASD by evaluating a person's behavior and development. ASD can usually be reliably diagnosed by the age of two. It is important to seek an evaluation as soon as

possible. The earlier ASD is diagnosed, the sooner treatments and services can begin.

Diagnosis in Young Children

Diagnosis in young children is often a two-stage process.

Stage 1: General Developmental Screening during Well-Child Checkups

Every child should receive well-child checkups with a pediatrician or an early childhood health-care provider. The American Academy of Pediatrics (AAP) recommends that all children receive screening for developmental delays at their 9-, 18-, and 24- or 30-month well-child visits, with specific autism screenings at their 18- and 24-month well-child visits. A child may receive additional screening if they have a higher likelihood of ASD or developmental problems. Children with a higher likelihood of ASD include those who have a family member with ASD, show some behaviors that are typical of ASD, have older parents, have certain genetic conditions, or had a very low birth weight.

Considering caregivers' experiences and concerns is an important part of the screening process for young children. The health-care provider may ask questions about the child's behaviors and evaluate those answers in combination with information from ASD screening tools and clinical observations of the child.

If a child shows developmental differences in behavior or functioning during this screening process, the health-care provider may refer the child for additional evaluation.

Stage 2: Additional Diagnostic Evaluation

It is important to accurately detect and diagnose children with ASD as early as possible, as this will shed light on their unique strengths and challenges. Early detection can also help caregivers determine which services, educational programs, and behavioral therapies are most likely to be helpful for their child.

A team of health-care providers who have experience diagnosing ASD will conduct the diagnostic evaluation. This team may include child neurologists, developmental pediatricians, speech-language pathologists, child psychologists and psychiatrists, educational specialists, and occupational therapists.

The diagnostic evaluation is likely to include the following:
- medical and neurological examinations
- assessment of the child's cognitive abilities
- assessment of the child's language abilities
- observation of the child's behavior
- an in-depth conversation with the child's caregivers about the child's behavior and development
- assessment of age-appropriate skills needed to complete daily activities independently, such as eating, dressing, and toileting

Because ASD is a complex disorder that sometimes occurs with other illnesses or learning disorders, the comprehensive evaluation may include the following:
- blood tests
- hearing test

The evaluation may lead to a formal diagnosis and recommendations for treatment.

Diagnosis in Older Children and Adolescents

Caregivers and teachers are often the first to recognize ASD symptoms in older children and adolescents who attend school. The school's special education team may perform an initial evaluation and then recommend that a child undergo additional evaluation with their primary health-care provider or a health-care provider who specializes in ASD.

A child's caregivers may talk with these health-care providers about their child's social difficulties, including problems with subtle communication. For example, some children may have problems understanding tone of voice, facial expressions, or body language. Older children and adolescents may have trouble understanding figures of speech, humor, or sarcasm. They may also have trouble forming friendships with peers.

Diagnosis in Adults

Diagnosing ASD in adults is often more difficult than diagnosing ASD in children. In adults, some ASD symptoms can overlap with symptoms of other mental health disorders, such as anxiety disorder or ADHD. Adults who notice signs of ASD should talk with a health-care provider and ask for a referral for an ASD evaluation. Although evaluation for ASD in adults is still being refined, adults may be referred to a neuropsychologist, psychologist, or psychiatrist who has experience with ASD. The expert will ask about:

- social interaction and communication challenges
- sensory issues
- repetitive behaviors
- restricted interests

The evaluation may also include a conversation with caregivers or other family members to learn about the person's early developmental history, which can help ensure an accurate diagnosis. Receiving a correct diagnosis of ASD as an adult can help a person understand past challenges, identify personal strengths, and find the right kind of help.

TREATMENTS AND THERAPIES FOR AUTISM SPECTRUM DISORDER

Treatment for ASD should begin as soon as possible after diagnosis. Early treatment for ASD is important as proper care and services can reduce individuals' difficulties while helping them build on their strengths and learn new skills. People with ASD may face a wide range of issues, which means that there is no single best treatment for ASD. Working closely with a health-care provider is an important part of finding the right combination of treatment and services.[2]

---

[2] "Autism Spectrum Disorder," National Institute of Mental Health (NIMH), February 1, 2024. Available online. URL: www.nimh.nih.gov/health/topics/autism-spectrum-disorders-asd#part_2283. Accessed February 6, 2024.

Chapter 10 | Cerebral Palsy

WHAT IS CEREBRAL PALSY?

Cerebral palsy (CP) is a group of disorders that affect a person's ability to move and maintain balance and posture. CP is the most common motor disability in childhood. Cerebral means having to do with the brain. Palsy means weakness or problems with using the muscles. CP is caused by abnormal brain development or damage to the developing brain that affects a person's ability to control his or her muscles.

The symptoms of CP vary from person to person. A person with severe CP might need to use special equipment to be able to walk or might not be able to walk at all and might need lifelong care. A person with mild CP, on the other hand, might walk a little awkwardly but might not need any special help. CP does not get worse over time though the exact symptoms can change over a person's lifetime. All people with CP have problems with movement and posture. Many also have related conditions, such as intellectual disability; seizures; problems with vision, hearing, or speech; changes in the spine (such as scoliosis); or joint problems (such as contractures).

CAUSES AND RISK FACTORS OF CEREBRAL PALSY

Cerebral palsy is caused by abnormal development of the brain or damage to the developing brain that affects a child's ability to control his or her muscles. There are several possible causes of the abnormal development or damage. People used to think that CP was mainly caused by a lack of oxygen during the birth process. Now, scientists think that this causes only a small number of CP cases.

The abnormal development of the brain or damage that leads to CP can happen before birth, during birth, within a month after birth, or during the first years of a child's life, while the brain is still developing. CP related to abnormal development of the brain or damage that occurred before or during birth is called "congenital CP." The majority of CP (85–90%) is congenital. In many cases, the specific cause is not known. A small percentage of CP is caused by abnormal development of the brain or damage that occurs more than 28 days after birth. This is called "acquired CP" and usually is associated with an infection (such as meningitis) or head injury.

EARLY SIGNS OF CEREBRAL PALSY

The signs of CP vary greatly because there are many different types and levels of disability. The main sign that a child might have CP is a delay reaching motor or movement milestones (such as rolling over, sitting, standing, or walking). Following are some other signs of possible CP. It is important to note that some children without CP might also have some of these signs.

In a Baby Younger than Six Months of Age

- His or her head lags when you pick him or her up while he or she is lying on his or her back.
- He or she feels stiff.
- He or she feels floppy.
- When held cradled in your arms, he or she seems to overextend his or her back and neck, constantly acting as if he or she is pushing away from you.
- When you pick him or her up, his or her legs get stiff, and they cross or scissors.

In a Baby Older than Six Months of Age

- He or she does not roll over in either direction.
- He or she cannot bring his or her hands together.
- He or she has difficulty bringing his or her hands to his or her mouth.
- He or she reaches out with only one hand while keeping the other fisted.

In a Baby Older than 10 Months of Age
- He or she crawls in a lopsided manner, pushing off with one hand and leg while dragging the opposite hand and leg.
- He or she scoots around on his or her buttocks or hops on his or her knees but does not crawl on all fours.

Tell your child's doctor or nurse if you notice any of these signs.

SCREENING AND DIAGNOSIS OF CEREBRAL PALSY
Developmental Monitoring
Developmental monitoring (also called "surveillance") means tracking a child's growth and development over time. At each well-child office visit, the doctor monitors the child's development. The doctor does this by asking parents if they have any concerns about their child's development, taking or updating the child's developmental history, and watching the child during the exam to see how he or she moves.

It is important for doctors to monitor the development of all children but especially those who are at a higher risk for developmental problems due to preterm birth or low birth weight. If any concerns about the child's development are raised during monitoring, then a developmental screening test should be given as soon as possible.

Developmental Screening
During developmental screening, a short test is given to see if the child has specific developmental delays, such as motor or movement delays. Some developmental screening tests are in the form of interviews or questionnaires completed by parents; others are tests that the doctor gives to the child. The American Academy of Pediatrics (AAP) recommends that all children be screened for developmental delays during regular well-child office visits at:
- nine months
- 18 months
- 24 or 30 months

Developmental and Medical Evaluations

The goal of a developmental evaluation is to diagnose the specific type of disorder that affects a child. To evaluate movement or motor delays, the doctor will look closely at the child's motor skills, muscle tone, reflexes, and posture and take a careful medical history from the parents. The doctor will try to rule out other disorders that could cause similar problems. Because many children with CP also have related developmental conditions such as intellectual disability, seizures, or vision, hearing, or speech problems, it is important to evaluate the child to find these disorders as well.

The developmental evaluation can be performed by the primary care doctor or by a specialist. Specialists who can do this type of developmental evaluation include the following:

- developmental pediatricians or neurodevelopment pediatricians (doctors with special training in child development and in evaluating children developmental problems)
- child neurologists (doctors with special training in childhood diseases of the brain, spine, and nerves)
- pediatric physiatrists or pediatric rehabilitation doctors (doctors with special training in physical medicine and rehabilitation for children)

TREATMENTS AND INTERVENTION SERVICES FOR CEREBRAL PALSY

There is no cure for CP, but treatment can improve the lives of those who have the condition. It is important to begin a treatment program as early as possible. After a CP diagnosis is made, a team of health professionals works with the child and family to develop a plan to help the child reach his or her full potential. Common treatments include medicines, surgery, braces, and physical, occupational, and speech therapy. No single treatment is the best one for all children with CP. Before deciding on a treatment plan, it is important to talk with the child's doctor to understand all the risks and benefits.

Intervention Services

Both early intervention and school-aged services are available through our nation's special education law—the Individuals with

Disabilities Education Act (IDEA). Part C of the IDEA deals with early intervention services (birth through 36 months of age), while Part B applies to services for school-aged children (3–21 years of age). Even if your child has not been diagnosed with CP, he or she may be eligible for IDEA services.

IF YOU ARE CONCERNED

If you think your child is not meeting movement milestones or might have CP, contact your doctor or nurse and share your concerns. If you or your doctor is still concerned, ask for a referral to a specialist who can do a more in-depth evaluation of your child and assist in making a diagnosis.

At the same time, call your state's public early childhood system to request a free evaluation to find out if your child qualifies for intervention services. This is sometimes called a "Child Find" evaluation.

Where to call for a free evaluation from the state depends on your child's age:

- **Your child is under age three.** Contact your local early intervention system. You can find the right contact information for your state by calling the Early Childhood Technical Assistance (ECTA) Center at 919-962-2001 or visiting the ECTA Center website (www.ectacenter.org/contact/ptccoord.asp).
- **Your child is aged three or older.** Contact your local public school system.

Even if your child is not yet old enough for kindergarten or enrolled in a public school, call your local elementary school or board of education and ask to speak with someone who can help you have your child evaluated. If you are not sure who to contact, you can call the ECTA Center at 919-962-2001 or visit the ECTA website: https://ectacenter.org/contact/ptccoord.asp.[1]

---

[1] National Center on Birth Defects and Developmental Disabilities (NCBDDD), "What Is Cerebral Palsy?" Centers for Disease Control and Prevention (CDC), February 28, 2024. Available online. URL: www.cdc.gov/ncbddd/cp/facts.html. Accessed February 29, 2024.

Chapter 11 | Birth Defects and Intellectual Disability

WHAT ARE BIRTH DEFECTS?
Birth defects are structural changes present at birth that can affect almost any part or parts of the body (e.g., heart, brain, and foot). They may affect how the body looks, works, or both. Birth defects can vary from mild to severe. The well-being of each child affected with a birth defect depends mostly on which organ or body part is involved and how much it is affected. Depending on the severity of the defect and what body part is affected, the expected life span of a person with a birth defect may or may not be affected.[1]

TYPES OF BIRTH DEFECTS
There are two main categories of congenital anomalies.

Structural Congenital Anomalies
Structural congenital anomalies are related to a problem with the structure of body parts. These can include the following:
- cleft lip or cleft palate
- heart defects, such as missing or misshaped valves
- atypical limbs, such as a clubfoot
- neural tube defects, such as spina bifida, and problems related to the growth and development of the brain and spinal cord

---

[1] National Center on Birth Defects and Developmental Disabilities (NCBDDD), "What Are Birth Defects?" Centers for Disease Control and Prevention (CDC), June 28, 2023. Available online. URL: www.cdc.gov/ncbddd/birthdefects/facts.html. Accessed February 6, 2024.

Functional or Developmental Congenital Anomalies

Functional or developmental congenital anomalies are related to a problem with how a body part or body system works or functions. These problems can include the following:

- **Nervous system or brain problems.** These include intellectual and developmental disabilities (IDDs), behavioral disorders, speech or language difficulties, seizures, and movement trouble. Some examples of congenital anomalies that affect the nervous system include Down syndrome, Prader-Willi syndrome (PWS), and fragile X syndrome (FXS).
- **Sensory problems.** Examples include hearing loss and visual problems, such as blindness or deafness.
- **Metabolic disorders.** These involve problems with certain chemical reactions in the body, such as conditions that limit the body's ability to rid itself of waste materials or harmful chemicals. Two common metabolic disorders are phenylketonuria (PKU) and hypothyroidism.
- **Degenerative disorders.** These are conditions that might not be obvious at birth but cause one or more aspects of health to steadily get worse. Examples of degenerative disorders are muscular dystrophy and X-linked adrenoleukodystrophy, which leads to problems of the nervous system and the adrenal glands and was the subject of the movie "Lorenzo's Oil."

Some congenital anomalies affect many parts or processes in the body, leading to both structural and functional problems.[2]

IDENTIFYING BIRTH DEFECTS

A birth defect can be found before birth, at birth, or any time after birth. Most birth defects are found within the first year of life. Some birth defects (such as cleft lip) are easy to see, but others (such as heart defects or hearing loss) are found using special tests, such

---

[2] "What Are the Types of Congenital Anomalies?" *Eunice Kennedy Shriver* National Institute of Child Health and Human Development (NICHD), December 21, 2023. Available online. URL: www.nichd.nih.gov/health/topics/congenital-anomalies/conditioninfo/types. Accessed February 6, 2024.

as echocardiograms (an ultrasound picture of the heart), x-rays, or hearing tests.

DIAGNOSIS OF BIRTH DEFECTS
Birth defects can be diagnosed during pregnancy or after the baby is born, depending on the specific type of birth defect.

During Pregnancy: Prenatal Testing
Screening Tests
A screening test is a procedure or test that is done to see if a woman or her baby might have certain problems. A screening test does not provide a specific diagnosis—that requires a diagnostic test. A screening test can sometimes give an abnormal result even when there is nothing wrong with the mother or her baby. Less often, a screening test result can be normal and miss a problem that does exist. During pregnancy, women are usually offered these screening tests to check for birth defects or other problems for the woman or her baby. Talk to your doctor about any concerns you have about prenatal testing.

Diagnostic Tests
If the result of a screening test is abnormal, doctors usually offer further diagnostic tests to determine if birth defects or other possible problems with the baby are present. These diagnostic tests are also offered to women with higher-risk pregnancies, which may include women who are aged 35 or older; women who have had a previous pregnancy affected by a birth defect; women who have chronic diseases such as lupus, high blood pressure, diabetes, or epilepsy; or women who use certain medications.

After the Baby Is Born
Certain birth defects might not be diagnosed until after the baby is born. Sometimes the birth defect is immediately seen at birth. For other birth defects, including some heart defects, the birth defect might not be diagnosed until later in life. When there is a health problem with a child, the primary care provider might look for birth defects by taking a medical and family history, doing a physical

exam, and sometimes recommending further tests. If a diagnosis cannot be made after the exam, the primary care provider might refer the child to a specialist in birth defects and genetics. A clinical geneticist is a doctor with special training to evaluate patients who may have genetic conditions or birth defects. Even if a child sees a specialist, an exact diagnosis might not be reached.

CAUSES OF BIRTH DEFECTS

Birth defects can occur during any stage of pregnancy. Most birth defects occur in the first three months of pregnancy when the organs of the baby are forming. This is a very important stage of development. However, some birth defects occur later in pregnancy. During the last six months of pregnancy, the tissues and organs continue to grow and develop.

For some birth defects, such as fetal alcohol syndrome (FAS), we know the cause. But, for most birth defects, we do not know what causes them. For most birth defects, we think they are caused by a complex mix of factors. These factors include our genes (information inherited from our parents), our behaviors, and things in the environment. But we do not fully understand how these factors might work together to cause birth defects. While we still have more work to do, we have learned a lot about birth defects through past research.

PREVENTION OF BIRTH DEFECTS

Not all birth defects can be prevented. But there are things that a woman can do before and during pregnancy to increase her chance of having a healthy baby:
- Be sure to see your health-care provider regularly and start prenatal care as soon as you think you might be pregnant.
- Get 400 micrograms (mcg) of folic acid every day, starting at least one month before getting pregnant.
- Do not drink alcohol or smoke.
- Talk to a health-care provider about any medications you are taking or thinking about taking. This includes prescription and over-the-counter (OTC) medications and dietary or herbal supplements. Do not stop or start taking any type of medication without first talking with a doctor.

- Know how to prevent infections during pregnancy.
- Be proactive in identifying and treating fever when ill or after getting a vaccine. Treat fevers higher than 101 °F (38.33 °C) with Tylenol® (or store-brand acetaminophen) and avoid hot tubs, saunas, or other environments that might cause overheating.
- If possible, be sure any medical conditions are under control, before becoming pregnant. Some conditions, such as diabetes, can increase the risk of birth defects.

LIVING WITH A BIRTH DEFECT

Babies who have birth defects often need special care and interventions to survive and to thrive developmentally. State birth defects tracking programs provide one way to identify and refer children as early as possible for services they need. Early intervention is vital to improving outcomes for these babies. If your child has a birth defect, you should ask his or her doctor about local resources and treatment. Geneticists, genetic counselors, and other specialists are another resource.[3]

WHAT IS INTELLECTUAL DISABILITY?

Intellectual disability is a term used when there are limits to a person's ability to learn at an expected level and function in daily life. Levels of intellectual disability vary greatly in children. Children with intellectual disability might have a hard time letting others know their wants and needs and taking care of themselves. Intellectual disability could cause a child to learn and develop more slowly than other children of the same age. It could take longer for a child with intellectual disability to learn to speak, walk, dress, or eat without help, and they could have trouble learning in school.

Intellectual disability can be caused by a problem that starts any time before a child turns 18 years old—even before birth. It can be caused by injury, disease, or a problem in the brain. For many children, the cause of their intellectual disability is not known. Some of the most commonly known causes of intellectual disability—such

---

[3] See Footnote [1].

as Down syndrome, FAS, FXS, genetic conditions, birth defects, and infections—happen before birth. Others happen while a baby is being born or soon after birth. Still, other causes of intellectual disability do not occur until a child is older; these might include serious head injury, stroke, or certain infections.

WHAT ARE SOME OF THE SIGNS OF INTELLECTUAL DISABILITY?

Usually, the more severe the degree of intellectual disability, the earlier the signs can be noticed. However, it might still be hard to tell how young children will be affected later in life. There are many signs of intellectual disability. For example, children with intellectual disability may:
- sit up, crawl, or walk later than other children
- learn to talk later or have trouble speaking
- find it hard to remember things
- have trouble understanding social rules
- have trouble seeing the results of their actions
- have trouble solving problems

WHAT CAN YOU DO IF YOU THINK YOUR CHILD MAY HAVE INTELLECTUAL DISABILITY?

Talk with your child's doctor or nurse. If you or your doctor thinks there could be a problem, you can take your child to see a developmental pediatrician or other specialist, and you can contact your local early intervention agency (for children under three) or public school (for children three and older). To find out whom to speak to in your area, you can contact the Parent Center in your state at www.parentcenterhub.org/find-yourcenter.[4]

---

[4] National Center on Birth Defects and Developmental Disabilities (NCBDDD), "Facts about Intellectual Disability," Centers for Disease Control and Prevention (CDC), May 10, 2022. Available online. URL: www.cdc.gov/ncbddd/developmentaldisabilities/facts-about-intellectual-disability.html. Accessed February 6, 2024.

Chapter 12 | Fetal Alcohol Spectrum Disorders

WHAT ARE FETAL ALCOHOL SPECTRUM DISORDERS?

Fetal alcohol spectrum disorders (FASDs) are a group of conditions that can occur in a person who was exposed to alcohol before birth. These effects can include physical problems and problems with behavior and learning. Often, a person with an FASD has a mix of these problems.

CAUSE AND PREVENTION OF FETAL ALCOHOL SPECTRUM DISORDERS

Fetal alcohol spectrum disorders can occur when a person is exposed to alcohol before birth. Alcohol in the mother's blood passes to the baby through the umbilical cord. There is no known safe amount of alcohol during pregnancy or when trying to get pregnant. There is also no safe time to drink during pregnancy. Alcohol can cause problems for a developing baby throughout pregnancy, including before a woman knows she is pregnant. All types of alcohol are equally harmful, including all wines and beer.

To prevent FASDs, a woman should avoid alcohol if she is pregnant or might be pregnant. This is because a woman could get pregnant and not know for up to four to six weeks. It is never too late to stop alcohol use during pregnancy. Because brain growth takes place throughout pregnancy, stopping alcohol use will improve the baby's health and well-being. FASDs are preventable if a baby is not exposed to alcohol before birth.

SIGNS AND SYMPTOMS OF FETAL ALCOHOL SPECTRUM DISORDERS

Fetal alcohol spectrum disorders refer to a collection of diagnoses that represent the range of effects that can happen to a person who was exposed to alcohol before birth. These conditions can affect each person in different ways and can range from mild to severe. A person with an FASD might have:
- low body weight
- poor coordination
- hyperactive behavior
- difficulty with attention
- poor memory
- difficulty in school (especially with math)
- learning disabilities
- speech and language delays
- intellectual disability or low intelligence quotient (IQ)
- poor reasoning and judgment skills
- sleep and sucking problems as a baby
- vision or hearing problems
- problems with the heart, kidneys, or bones
- shorter-than-average height
- small head size
- abnormal facial features, such as a smooth ridge between the nose and upper lip (This ridge is called the "philtrum.")

DIAGNOSIS OF FETAL ALCOHOL SPECTRUM DISORDERS

Different FASD diagnoses are based on particular symptoms and include the following:
- **Fetal alcohol syndrome (FAS).** The FAS represents the most involved end of the FASD spectrum. People with FAS have central nervous system (CNS) problems, minor facial features, and growth problems. People with FAS can have problems with learning, memory, attention span, communication, vision, or hearing. They might have a mix of these problems. People with FAS

often have a hard time in school and trouble getting along with others.
- **Alcohol-related neurodevelopmental disorder (ARND).** People with ARND might have intellectual disabilities and problems with behavior and learning. They might do poorly in school and have difficulties with math, memory, attention, judgment, and poor impulse control.
- **Alcohol-related birth defects (ARBD).** People with ARBD might have problems with the heart, kidneys, or bones or with hearing. They might have a mix of these.
- **Neurobehavioral disorder associated with prenatal alcohol exposure (ND-PAE).** The ND-PAE was first included as a recognized condition in the *Diagnostic and Statistical Manual-5* (*DSM 5*) of the American Psychiatric Association (APA) in 2013. A child or youth with ND-PAE will have problems in the following three areas:
  - thinking and memory, where the child may have trouble planning or may forget material he or she has already learned
  - behavior problems, such as severe tantrums, mood issues (e.g., irritability), and difficulty shifting attention from one task to another
  - trouble with day-to-day living, which can include problems with bathing, dressing for the weather, and playing with other children

In addition, to be diagnosed with ND-PAE, the mother of the child must have consumed more than minimal levels of alcohol before the child's birth, which the American Psychological Association (APA) defines as more than 13 alcoholic drinks per month of pregnancy (i.e., any 30-day period of pregnancy) or more than two alcoholic drinks in one sitting.

Areas Evaluated for Fetal Alcohol Spectrum Disorder Diagnoses

The term FASDs is not meant for use as a clinical diagnosis. Diagnosing FASDs can be hard because there is no medical test, such as a blood test, for these conditions. And other disorders, such as attention deficit hyperactivity disorder (ADHD) and Williams syndrome (WS), have some symptoms such as FAS.

To diagnose FASDs, doctors look for:
- prenatal alcohol exposure, although confirmation is not required to make a diagnosis
- CNS problems (e.g., small head size, problems with attention and hyperactivity, and poor coordination)
- lower-than-average height, weight, or both
- abnormal facial features (e.g., the smooth ridge between the nose and upper lip)

TREATMENT OF FETAL ALCOHOL SPECTRUM DISORDERS

Fetal alcohol spectrum disorders last a lifetime. There is no cure for FASDs, but research shows that early intervention treatment services can improve a child's development. There are many types of treatment options, including medication to help with some symptoms, behavior and education therapy, parent training, and other alternative approaches. No one treatment is right for every child. Good treatment plans will include close monitoring, follow-ups, and changes as needed along the way. Also, "protective factors" can help reduce the effects of FASDs and help people with these conditions reach their full potential. Protective factors include the following:
- diagnosis before six years of age
- loving, nurturing, and stable home environment during the school years
- absence of violence
- involvement in special education and social services

GET HELP

If you or the doctor thinks there could be a problem, ask the doctor for a referral to a specialist (someone who knows about FASDs), such as a developmental pediatrician, child psychologist, or clinical geneticist. In some cities, there are clinics whose staff have special training in diagnosing and treating children with FASDs. To find doctors and clinics in your area, visit the National Resource

Directory (NRD; https://fasdunited.org/resource-directory) from FASD United (formerly the National Organization on Fetal Alcohol Syndrome (NOFAS)).

At the same time as you ask the doctor for a referral to a specialist, call your state or territory's early intervention program to request a free evaluation to find out if your child can get services to help. This is sometimes called a "Child Find" evaluation. You do not need to wait for a doctor's referral or a medical diagnosis to make this call. Where to call for a free evaluation from the state depends on your child's age:

- **Your child is under age three.** Call your state or territory's early intervention program (www.cdc.gov/ncbddd/actearly/parents/states.html) and say, "I have concerns about my child's development, and I would like to have my child evaluated to find out if he/she is eligible for early intervention services."
- **Your child is aged three or older.** Contact your local public school system. Even if your child is not old enough for kindergarten or enrolled in a public school, call your local elementary school or board of education and ask to speak with someone who can help you have your child evaluated.[1]

---

[1] National Center on Birth Defects and Developmental Disabilities (NCBDDD), "Basics about FASDs," Centers for Disease Control and Prevention (CDC), October 3, 2023. Available online. URL: www.cdc.gov/ncbddd/fasd/facts.html. Accessed February 6, 2024.

Chapter 13 | Hearing and Vision Loss

WHAT IS HEARING LOSS?
Hearing loss can happen when any part of the ear is not working in the usual way. This includes the outer ear, middle ear, inner ear, hearing (acoustic) nerve, and auditory system. Hearing loss can affect a child's ability to develop speech, language, and social skills. The earlier children with hearing loss start getting services, the more likely they are to reach their full potential. If you think that a child might have hearing loss, ask the child's doctor for a hearing screening as soon as possible.

Causes and Risk Factors of Hearing Loss
Hearing loss can happen at any time during life—from before birth to adulthood. Following are some of the things that can increase the chance that a child will have hearing loss:
- One out of two cases of hearing loss in babies is due to genetic causes. Some babies with a genetic cause for their hearing loss might have family members who also have hearing loss. About one out of three babies with genetic hearing loss has a "syndrome." This means they have other conditions in addition to the hearing loss, such as Down syndrome or Usher syndrome.
- One out of four cases of hearing loss in babies is due to maternal infections during pregnancy, complications after birth, and head trauma. For example, the child:
  - was exposed to infection, such as, before birth
  - spent five days or more in a hospital neonatal intensive care unit (NICU) or had complications while in the NICU

- needed a special procedure, such as a blood transfusion, to treat bad jaundice
- had head, face, or ears shaped or formed in a different way than usual
- had a condition, such as a neurological disorder, that may be associated with hearing loss
- had an infection around the brain and spinal cord called "meningitis"
- received a bad injury to the head that required a hospital stay

Signs and Symptoms of Hearing Loss

The signs and symptoms of hearing loss are different for each child. If you think that your child might have hearing loss, ask the child's doctor for a hearing screening as soon as possible. Even if a child has passed a hearing screening before, it is important to look out for the following signs.

Signs in Babies
- Does not startle at loud noises.
- Does not turn to the source of a sound after six months of age.
- Does not say single words, such as "dada" or "mama," by one year of age.
- Turns head when he or she sees you but not if you only call out his or her name. This is sometimes mistaken for not paying attention or just ignoring but could be the result of a partial or complete hearing loss.
- Seems to hear some sounds but not others.

Signs in Children
- Speech is delayed.
- Speech is not clear.
- Does not follow directions. This is sometimes mistaken for not paying attention or just ignoring but could be the result of a partial or complete hearing loss.
- Often says, "Huh?"
- Turns the television volume up too high.

Babies and children should reach milestones in how they play, learn, communicate, and act. A delay in any of these milestones could be a sign of hearing loss or other developmental problems.

Screening and Diagnosis in Hearing Loss
Hearing screening can tell if a child might have hearing loss. Hearing screening is easy and is not painful. In fact, babies are often asleep while being screened. It takes a very short time—usually only a few minutes.

Babies
All babies should have a hearing screening no later than one month of age. Most babies have their hearing screened while still in the hospital. If a baby does not pass a hearing screening, it is very important to get a full hearing test as soon as possible but no later than three months of age.

Children
Children should have their hearing tested before they enter school or any time there is a concern about the child's hearing. Children who do not pass the hearing screening need to get a full hearing test as soon as possible.

Hearing Loss Treatments and Intervention Services
No single treatment or intervention is the answer for every person or family. Good treatment plans will include close monitoring, follow-ups, and any changes needed along the way. There are many different types of communication options for children with hearing loss and for their families. Some of these options include the following:
- learning other ways to communicate, such as sign language
- technology to help with communication, such as hearing aids and cochlear implants
- medicine and surgery to correct some types of hearing loss
- family support services

Prevention of Hearing Loss

Following are tips for parents to help prevent hearing loss in their children:
- Have a healthy pregnancy.
- Make sure your child gets all the regular childhood vaccines.
- Keep your child away from high noise levels, such as from very loud toys.

Getting Help

- If you think that your child might have hearing loss, ask the child's doctor for a hearing screening as soon as possible.
- If your child does not pass a hearing screening, ask the child's doctor for a full hearing test as soon as possible.
- If your child has hearing loss, talk to the child's doctor about treatment and intervention services.

Hearing loss can affect a child's ability to develop speech, language, and social skills. The earlier children with hearing loss start getting services, the more likely they are to reach their full potential. If you are a parent and you suspect your child has hearing loss, trust your instincts and speak with your child's doctor.[1]

WHAT IS VISION LOSS?

Vision loss means that a person's eyesight is not corrected to a "normal" level. Vision loss can vary greatly among children and can be caused by many things.

What Causes Loss of Vision?

Vision loss can be caused by damage to the eye itself, by the eye being shaped incorrectly, or even by a problem in the brain. Babies can be born unable to see, and vision loss can occur anytime during a person's life.

---

[1] National Center on Birth Defects and Developmental Disabilities (NCBDDD), "What Is Hearing Loss in Children?" Centers for Disease Control and Prevention (CDC), August 4, 2023. Available online. URL: www.cdc.gov/ncbddd/hearingloss/facts.html. Accessed February 6, 2024.

What Are Some Signs of Vision Loss?
A child with vision loss might:
- close or cover one eye
- squint the eyes or frown
- complain that things are blurry or hard to see
- have trouble reading or doing other close-up work or hold objects close to eyes in order to see
- blink more than usual or seem cranky when doing close-up work (such as looking at books)

One eye of a child with vision loss could look out or cross. One or both eyes could be watery, and one or both of the child's eyelids could also look red-rimmed, crusted, or swollen.

When Should Your Child Be Checked?
- newborn to three months
- six months to one year
- about three years
- about five years

Having your child's vision checked is especially important if someone in your family has had vision problems.

What Can You Do If You Think Your Child May Have Vision Loss?
Treating vision problems early may protect your child's sight, and teaching children with severe vision loss how to function as early as possible can help them reach their full potential.[2]

SEE, HEAR, SPEAK
Nearly all newborns are screened for hearing loss before leaving the hospital. For newborns diagnosed with hearing loss, interventions such as hearing aids or cochlear implants should begin no later than six months of age. When interventions begin early, children with hearing loss can develop language skills that help them communicate.

---

[2] National Center on Birth Defects and Developmental Disabilities (NCBDDD), "Facts about Vision Loss in Children," Centers for Disease Control and Prevention (CDC), February 23, 2023. Available online. URL: www.cdc.gov/ncbddd/childdevelopment/facts-about-vision-loss.html. Accessed February 6, 2024.

Hearing problems can also arise in older kids. "Some children are born with normal hearing and develop hearing loss later for various reasons," says Dr. Mary Pat Moeller, director of the Center for Childhood Deafness at Boys Town National Research Hospital, Omaha, Nebraska. Head injuries, meningitis, and chronic fluid behind the eardrum from repeated bouts of ear infections are just a few conditions that can lead to later hearing loss.

The study evaluated different tests and identified a few that could best detect vision problems—even when performed by people who are not vision specialists. Screenings only identify potential problems, and they do not catch everything. Children should have regular exams by an eye care professional. Early detection and treatment of hearing, vision, and language problems can give kids a better learning experience.[3]

---

[3] *NIH News in Health,* "See, Hear, Speak," National Institutes of Health (NIH), September 2012. Available online. URL: https://newsinhealth.nih.gov/2012/09/see-hear-speak. Accessed February 6, 2024.

Chapter 14 | Genetic Disorders and Learning Disability

A genetic disorder is a disease caused in whole or in part by a change in the deoxyribonucleic acid (DNA) sequence away from the normal sequence. Genetic disorders can be caused by a mutation in one gene (monogenic disorder), by mutations in multiple genes (multifactorial inheritance disorder), by a combination of gene mutations and environmental factors, or by damage to chromosomes (changes in the number or structure of entire chromosomes, the structures that carry genes).

As the secrets of the human genome are unlocked (the complete set of human genes), it comes to know that nearly all diseases have a genetic component. Some diseases are caused by mutations that are inherited from the parents and are present in an individual at birth, such as sickle cell disease. Other diseases are caused by acquired mutations in a gene or group of genes that occur during a person's life. Such mutations are not inherited from a parent but occur either randomly or due to some environmental exposure (such as cigarette smoke). These include many cancers as well as some forms of neurofibromatosis.[1]

WHAT IS FRAGILE X SYNDROME?

Fragile X syndrome (FXS) is a genetic disorder. FXS is caused by changes in a gene called "*Fragile X Messenger Ribonucleoprotein 1*" (*FMR1*). *FMR1* usually makes a protein called the "Fragile X mental retardation protein" (FMRP) that is needed for brain development.

---

[1] "Genetic Disorders," National Human Genome Research Institute (NHGRI), May 18, 2018. Available online. URL: www.genome.gov/For-Patients-and-Families/Genetic-Disorders. Accessed February 18, 2024.

People who have FXS do not make this protein. Those with fragile X-associated disorders have changes in the *FMR1* gene but usually still make some of the protein.

FXS affects both males and females. However, females often have milder symptoms than males. The exact number of people who have FXS is unknown, but a review of research studies estimated that about 1 in 7,000 males and about 1 in 11,000 females have been diagnosed with FXS.

Signs and Symptoms of Fragile X Syndrome
Signs that a child might have FXS include the following:
- developmental delays (not sitting, walking, or talking at the same time as other children the same age)
- learning disabilities (trouble learning new skills)
- social and behavior problems (such as not making eye contact, anxiety, trouble paying attention, hand flapping, acting and speaking without thinking, and being very active)

Males who have FXS usually have some degree of intellectual disability that can range from mild to severe. Females with FXS can have normal intelligence or some degree of intellectual disability. Autism spectrum disorder (ASD) also occurs more frequently in people with FXS.

Testing and Diagnosis of Fragile X Syndrome
FXS can be diagnosed by testing a person's DNA from a blood test. A doctor or genetic counselor can order the test. Testing can also be done to find changes in the *FMR1* gene that can lead to fragile X-associated disorders. A diagnosis of FXS can be helpful to the family because it can provide a reason for a child's intellectual disabilities and behavior problems. This allows the family and other caregivers to learn more about the disorder and manage care so that the child can reach his or her full potential. However, the results of DNA tests can affect other family members and raise many issues. So anyone who is thinking about FXS testing should consider having genetic counseling prior to getting tested.

Treatments of Fragile X Syndrome

There is no cure for FXS. However, treatment services can help people learn important skills. Services can include therapy to learn to talk, walk, and interact with others. In addition, medicine can be used to help control some issues, such as behavior problems. To develop the best treatment plan, people with FXS, parents, and health-care providers should work closely with one another and with everyone involved in treatment and support—which may include teachers, childcare providers, coaches, therapists, and other family members.

Early Intervention Services

Early intervention services help children from birth to three years old (36 months) learn important skills. These services may improve a child's development. Even if the child has not been diagnosed with FXS, they may be eligible for services. These services are provided through an early intervention system in each state. Through this system, you can ask for an evaluation. In addition, treatment for particular symptoms, such as speech therapy for language delays, often does not need to wait for a formal diagnosis. While early intervention is extremely important, treatment services at any age can be helpful.

What to Do If You Think Your Child Might Have Fragile X Syndrome

Local public school systems can provide services and support for children aged three and older. Children can access some services even if they do not attend public school. When parents are concerned about a child's development, it can be very challenging for them to figure out the right steps to take. States have created parent centers. These centers help families learn how and where to have their children evaluated and how to find services.

Finding Support

Having support and community resources can help increase confidence in managing FXS, enhance quality of life, and assist in meeting the needs of all family members. It might be helpful for parents of children with FXS to talk with one another. One parent might have learned how to address some of the same concerns another parent has. Often, parents of children with special needs can give advice about good resources for these children.

Remember that the choices of one family might not be best for another family, so it is important that parents understand all options and discuss them with their child's health-care providers.

- Contact the National Fragile X Foundation at 1-800-688-8765 or treatment@fragileX.org to get information about treatments, educational strategies, therapies, and intervention.
- Connect with a Community Support Network (CSN) at the National Fragile X Foundation. CSNs are organized and run by parent volunteers and provide support to families.[2]

WHAT IS DOWN SYNDROME?

Down syndrome is a condition in which a person has an extra chromosome or an extra piece of a chromosome. This extra copy changes how a baby's body and brain develop. It can cause both mental and physical challenges during their lifetime. Even though people with Down syndrome might act and look similar, each person has different abilities.

What Causes Down Syndrome?

Chromosomes are tiny "packages" in your cells that contain your genes. Genes carry information, called "DNA," that controls what you look like and how your body works. People with Down syndrome have an extra copy of chromosome 21. In some cases, they may have an extra copy of part of the chromosome. Having an extra copy of a chromosome is called "trisomy." So sometimes Down syndrome is also called "trisomy 21."

---

[2] National Center on Birth Defects and Developmental Disabilities (NCBDDD), "What Is Fragile X Syndrome?" Centers for Disease Control and Prevention (CDC), June 3, 2022. Available online. URL: www.cdc.gov/ncbddd/fxs/facts.html. Accessed February 18, 2024.

Down syndrome is usually not inherited. It happens by chance, as an error when cells are dividing during the early development of the fetus. It is not known for sure why Down syndrome occurs or how many different factors play a role. One factor that increases the risk of having a baby with Down syndrome is the age of the mother. Women aged 35 and older are more likely to have a baby with Down syndrome.

What Are the Symptoms of Down Syndrome?
The symptoms of Down syndrome are different in each person. And people with Down syndrome may have different problems at different times of their lives. They usually have mild-to-moderate intellectual disabilities. Their development is often delayed. For example, they may start talking later than other children.

How Is Down Syndrome Diagnosed?
Health-care providers can check for Down syndrome during pregnancy or after a child is born. There are two basic types of tests that help find Down syndrome during pregnancy:
- **Prenatal screening tests.** These tests can show whether your unborn baby has a higher or lower chance of having Down syndrome. If a screening test shows that your baby could have Down syndrome, you will need another test to find out for sure.
- **Prenatal diagnostic tests.** These tests can diagnose or rule out Down syndrome by checking the chromosomes in a sample of cells.

These tests have a small risk of causing a miscarriage, so they are often done after a screening test shows that an unborn baby could have Down syndrome.

After a baby is born, the provider may make an initial diagnosis of Down syndrome based on the physical signs of the syndrome. The provider can use a karyotype genetic test to confirm the diagnosis. The test can check for extra chromosomes in a sample of the baby's blood.

What Are the Treatments for Down Syndrome?

There is no single, standard treatment for Down syndrome. Treatments are based on each person's physical and intellectual needs, strengths, and limitations. Services early in life focus on helping children with Down syndrome develop to their full potential. These services include speech, occupational, and physical therapies. They are typically offered through early intervention programs in each state. Children with Down syndrome may also need extra help or attention in school although many children are included in regular classes. Since people with Down syndrome can have birth defects and other health problems, they will need regular medical care. They may need to have certain extra health screenings to check for problems that happen more often in people with Down syndrome.[3]

The following information may be helpful for those considering educational assistance programs for a child with Down syndrome:

- The child must have certain cognitive or learning deficits to be eligible for free special education programs. Parents can contact a local school principal or special education coordinator to learn how to have a child examined to see if he or she qualifies for services under the Individuals with Disabilities Education Act (IDEA).
- If a child qualifies for special services, a team of people will work together to design an Individualized Education Plan (IEP) for the child.
- The team may include parents or caregivers, teachers, a school psychologist, and other specialists in child development or education.
- The IEP includes specific learning goals for that child, based on their needs and capabilities. The team also decides how best to carry out the IEP.
- Children with Down syndrome may attend a school for children with special needs. Parents may have a choice between a school where most of the children do not have disabilities and one for children with special needs.

---

[3] MedlinePlus, "Down Syndrome," National Institutes of Health (NIH), January 26, 2024. Available online. URL: https://medlineplus.gov/downsyndrome.html. Accessed February 18, 2024.

Educators and health-care providers can help families with the decision about what environment is best. Integration into a regular school has become much more common in recent decades, and the IDEA requires that public schools work to maximize a child's access to typical learning experiences and interactions.[4]

WHAT IS TRIPLE X SYNDROME?

Triple X syndrome, also called "trisomy X" or "47,XXX," is characterized by the presence of an additional X chromosome in each of a female's cells. Although females with this condition may be taller than average, this chromosomal change typically causes no unusual physical features. Most females with trisomy X have normal sexual development and are able to conceive children.

Triple X syndrome is associated with an increased risk of learning disabilities and delayed development of speech and language skills. Delayed development of motor skills (such as sitting and walking), weak muscle tone (hypotonia), and behavioral and emotional difficulties are also possible, but these characteristics vary widely. Seizures or kidney abnormalities occur in about 10 percent of affected females.

Frequency of Triple X Syndrome

This condition occurs in about 1 in 1,000 female newborns; however, many of these affected individuals are never diagnosed. Five to ten people with trisomy X are born in the United States each day.

Causes of Triple X Syndrome

People normally have 46 chromosomes in each cell. Two of the 46 chromosomes, known as "X" and "Y," are called "sex chromosomes" because they help determine whether a person will develop male or female sex characteristics. Females typically have two X chromosomes (46,XX), and males have one X chromosome and one Y chromosome (46,XY).

---

[4] "What Are Common Treatments for Down Syndrome?" *Eunice Kennedy Shriver* National Institute of Child Health and Human Development (NICHD), February 16, 2024. Available online. URL: www.nichd.nih.gov/health/topics/down/conditioninfo/treatments. Accessed February 18, 2024.

Trisomy X results from an extra copy of the X chromosome in each of a female's cells. As a result of the extra X chromosome, each cell has a total of 47 chromosomes (47,XXX) instead of the usual 46. An extra copy of the X chromosome is associated with tall stature, learning problems, and other features in some affected individuals. Some females with trisomy X have an extra X chromosome in only some of their cells. This phenomenon is called "46,XX/47,XXX mosaicism."[5]

---

[5] MedlinePlus, "Trisomy X," National Institutes of Health (NIH), February 28, 2022. Available online. URL: https://medlineplus.gov/genetics/condition/trisomy-x. Accessed February 18, 2024.

Part 4 | Providing Support and Promoting Independence

Chapter 15 | Addressing Concerns about Child Development

TALK TO YOUR CHILD'S DOCTOR
As a parent, you know your child best. If your child is not meeting the milestones for his or her age or if you think there could be a problem with the way your child plays, learns, speaks, acts, and moves, talk to your child's doctor and share your concerns.

Complete a Milestone Checklist for Your Child's Age
- Use the Milestone Tracker app (www.cdc.gov/ncbddd/actearly/milestones-app.html) or fill out a milestone checklist to track your child's development. Share the completed checklist with your child's health-care provider. It is to be noted that these checklists are not a substitute for standardized, validated developmental screening tools.
- Read the tip sheet How to Get Help for Your Child (www.cdc.gov/ncbddd/actearly/pdf/help_pdfs/How-to-Get-Help-for-Your-Child_CombinedPDF_EngSpn-2-15-20_508.pdf) for steps you can take to help you act on developmental concerns.
- Watch a video (www.youtube.com/watch?v=uD68lmY-9TWI) in American Sign Language (ASL) on what to do if you have concerns about your child's development.

Ask about Developmental Screening
The American Academy of Pediatrics (AAP) recommends that children be screened for general development using standardized,

validated tools at 9, 18, or 30 months and for autism at 18 and 24 months or whenever a parent or provider has a concern. Ask the doctor about your child's developmental screening.

ASK FOR A REFERRAL

If you or the doctor thinks there might be a delay, ask the doctor for a referral to a specialist who can do a more in-depth evaluation of your child. Doctors your child might be referred to include the following:

- **Developmental pediatricians.** These doctors have special training in child development and children with special needs.
- **Child neurologists.** These doctors work on the brain, spine, and nerves.
- **Child psychologists or psychiatrists.** These doctors know about the human mind.

GET AN EVALUATION

At the same time as you ask the doctor for a referral to a specialist, call your state's public early childhood system to request a free evaluation to find out if your child qualifies for intervention services. This is sometimes called a "Child Find" evaluation. You do not need to wait for a doctor's referral or a medical diagnosis to make this call. Where to call for a free evaluation from the state depends on your child's age.

Children Aged Zero to Three

If your child is under the age of three, contact your local early intervention system.

Children Aged Three or Older

If your child is aged three or older, call any local public elementary school (even if your child does not go to school there) and say: "I have concerns about my child's development, and I would like to have my child evaluated through the school system for preschool special education services." If the person who answers is unfamiliar

Addressing Concerns about Child Development | 115

with preschool special education, ask to speak with the school or district's special education director.

MORE TIPS FOR PARENTS
Why Act Early?
If you are concerned about your child's development, do not wait. Acting early on developmental concerns can make a real difference for your child and you.

What to Say
If you are not sure what to say when you talk with your child's doctor or when you call to request an evaluation, visit the website www.cdc.gov/ncbddd/actearly/concerned-whattosay.html for some tips.

While You Wait
If you have to wait to get an appointment to see a specialist or start intervention services, know that there are some simple things you can do today and every day to help your child's development. Interact with your child as much as possible. Read books, sing songs, play with toys, make crafts, do household chores, and play outside together. Talk to your child: label items, point out interesting things, tell stories, comment about what you see and how you feel, and explain how things work and why things happen. Your child may not always seem to be listening, but he or she may be hearing more than you think.

Recordkeeping Worksheet
Use this recordkeeping worksheet (www.parentcenterhub.org/recordkeeping) to help you keep track of your notes.[1]

---

[1] National Center on Birth Defects and Developmental Disabilities (NCBDDD), "Concerned about Your Child's Development?" Centers for Disease Control and Prevention (CDC), June 6, 2023. Available online. URL: www.cdc.gov/ncbddd/actearly/concerned.html. Accessed February 7, 2024.

WHAT ARE YOUR CHILDCARE OPTIONS?

Before you start your childcare search, you may find it helpful to learn about all the childcare options that may be available. You want what is best for your child, so it is important to find a provider that fits your child's and family's needs. This means considering things such as the size of the program, the type of physical environment it provides (such as a home environment versus a classroom setting), the hours when it is available, and so on. The following are the types of childcare options, including how each option may be regulated to ensure your child's health and safety:

- childcare centers
- family childcare homes
- head start and early head start
- prekindergarten programs
- school-age childcare programs
- childcare options for military families
- informal in-home childcare[2]

---

[2] ChildCare.gov, "What Are My Child Care Options?" Administration for Children and Families (ACF), December 26, 2022. Available online. URL: https://childcare.gov/consumer-education/childcare-options. Accessed February 7, 2024.

Chapter 16 | Early Intervention Strategies

If you are concerned about the development of an infant or toddler or you suspect that a little one has a disability, this will summarize one terrific source of help—the early intervention system in your state. Early intervention services can help infants and toddlers with disabilities or delays to learn many key skills and catch up in their development. There is a lot to know about early intervention.

WHAT IS EARLY INTERVENTION?

Early intervention is a system of services that helps babies and toddlers with developmental delays or disabilities. Early intervention focuses on helping eligible babies and toddlers learn the basic and brand-new skills that typically develop during the first three years of life, such as:
- physical (reaching, rolling, crawling, and walking)
- cognitive (thinking, learning, and solving problems)
- communication (talking, listening, and understanding)
- social/emotional (playing and feeling secure and happy)
- self-help (eating and dressing)

Examples of Early Intervention Services

If an infant or toddler has a disability or a developmental delay in one or more of these developmental areas, that child will likely be eligible for early intervention services. Those services will be tailored to meet the child's individual needs and may include the following:
- assistive technology (devices a child might need)
- audiology or hearing services

- speech and language services
- counseling and training for a family
- medical services
- nursing services
- nutrition services
- occupational therapy
- physical therapy
- psychological services

Services may also be provided to address the needs and priorities of the child's family. Family-directed services are meant to help family members understand the special needs of their child and how to enhance his or her development.

Authorized by Law

Early intervention is available in every state and territory of the United States. The Individuals with Disabilities Education Act (IDEA) requires it—Part C of the IDEA, to be precise. That is why you will sometimes hear early intervention referred to as Part C.

WHO IS ELIGIBLE FOR EARLY INTERVENTION?

Early intervention is intended for infants and toddlers who have a developmental delay or disability. Eligibility is determined by evaluating the child (with parents' consent) to see if the little one does, in fact, have a delay in development or a disability. Eligible children can receive early intervention services from birth through the third birthday (and sometimes beyond).

- **For some children, from birth.** Sometimes it is known from the moment a child is born that early intervention services will be essential in helping the child grow and develop. Often, this is so for children who are diagnosed at birth with a specific condition or who experience significant prematurity, very low birth weight, illness, or surgery soon after being born. Even before heading home from the hospital, this child's parents may be given a referral to their local early intervention office.

- **For others, because of delays in development.** Some children have a relatively routine entry into the world but may develop more slowly than others, experience setbacks, or develop in ways that seem very different from other children. For these children, a visit with a developmental pediatrician and a thorough evaluation may lead to an early intervention referral.

Parents do not have to wait for a referral to early intervention, however. If you are concerned about your child's development, you may contact your local program directly and ask to have your child evaluated. That evaluation is provided free of charge. However, a child comes to be referred, evaluated, and determined eligible, early intervention services provide vital support so that children with developmental needs can thrive and grow.

WHAT IS A DEVELOPMENTAL DELAY?

The term "developmental delay" is an important one in early intervention. Broadly speaking, it means that a child is delayed in some area of development. There are five areas in which development may be affected:
- cognitive development
- physical development, including vision and hearing
- communication development
- social or emotional development
- adaptive development

Definition of "Developmental Delay"

Part C of the IDEA broadly defines the term "developmental delay." But the exact meaning of the term varies from state to state because each state defines the term for itself, including the following:
- describing the evaluation and assessment procedures that will be used to measure a child's development in each of the five developmental areas
- specifying the level of delay in functioning (or other comparable criteria) that constitutes a developmental delay in each of the five developmental areas

What Is Your State's Definition?

To find out how your state defines the term "developmental delay," you can ask your child's pediatrician or the local health department. Most likely, the definition is also online, so you can also "search" for it, making sure to include the name of your state in the search.

IF YOU ARE CONCERNED ABOUT A BABY OR TODDLER'S DEVELOPMENT

If you think that your child is not developing at the same pace or in the same way as most children his or her age, it is often a good idea to talk first to your child's pediatrician. Explain your concerns. Tell the doctor what you have observed with your child. Your child may have a disability or a developmental delay, or he or she may be at risk of having a disability or delay.

You can also get in touch with your community's early intervention program and ask to have your little one evaluated to see if he or she has a developmental delay or disability. This evaluation is free of charge, will not hurt your child, and looks at his or her basic skills. Based on that evaluation, your child may be eligible for early intervention services, which will be designed to address your child's special needs or delays.

- **How to get in touch with your community's early intervention program.** There are several ways to connect with the early intervention program in your community. Try any of the following suggestions:
  - Contact the pediatrics branch in a local hospital and ask where you should call to find out about early intervention services in your area.
  - Ask your pediatrician for a referral to the local early intervention system.
  - Visit the Economic Cooperation and Trade Agreement (ECTA) Center's early intervention "contacts" page available at http://ectacenter.org/contact/ptccoord.asp.
- **What to say to the early intervention contact person.** Explain that you are concerned about your child's development. Say that you think your child may need early

intervention services. Explain that you would like to have your child evaluated under Part C of the IDEA.
- **Referral.** Write down any information the contact person gives you. You will probably be referred either to your community's early intervention program or to what is known as "Child Find." Child Find operates in every state to identify babies and toddlers who need early intervention services because of developmental delays or disabilities. You can use the parent's record-keeping worksheet (www.parentcenterhub.org/wp-content/uploads/repo_items/recordkeeping.pdf) to keep track of this important information. In fact, in general, it is a good idea to write down the names and phone numbers of everyone you talk to as you move through the early intervention process.

THE EVALUATION AND ASSESSMENT PROCESS
- **Service coordinator.** Once connected with either Child Find or your community's early intervention program, you will be assigned a service coordinator who will explain the early intervention process and help you through the next steps in that process. The service coordinator will serve as your single point of contact with the early intervention system.
- **Screening and/or evaluation.** One of the first things that will happen is that your child will be evaluated to see if, indeed, he or she has a developmental delay or disability. (In some states, there may be a preliminary step called "screening" to see if there is cause to suspect that a baby or toddler has a disability or developmental delay.) The family's service coordinator will explain what is involved in the screening and/or evaluation and ask for your permission to proceed. You must provide your written consent before screening and/or evaluation may take place.

The evaluation group will be made up of qualified people who have different areas of training and experience. Together, they know about children's speech and language skills, physical abilities, hearing and vision, and other important areas of development. They know how to work with children, even very young ones, to discover if a child has a problem or is developing within normal ranges. Group members may evaluate your child together or individually. As part of the evaluation, the team will observe your child, ask your child to do things, talk to you and your child, and use other methods to gather information. These procedures will help the team find out how your child functions in the five areas of development.

- **Exceptions for diagnosed physical or mental conditions.** It is important to note that an evaluation of your child will not be necessary if he or she is automatically eligible due to a diagnosed physical or mental condition that has a high probability of resulting in a developmental delay. Such conditions include but are not limited to chromosomal abnormalities, genetic or congenital disorders, sensory impairments, inborn errors of metabolism, disorders reflecting disturbance of the development of the nervous system, congenital infections, severe attachment disorders, and disorders secondary to exposure to toxic substances, including fetal alcohol syndrome (FAS). Many states have policies that further specify what conditions automatically qualify an infant or toddler for early intervention (e.g., Down syndrome and fragile X syndrome (FXS)).
- **Determining eligibility.** The results of the evaluation will be used to determine your child's eligibility for early intervention services. You and a team of professionals will meet and review all of the data, results, and reports. The people on the team will talk with you about whether your child meets the criteria under the IDEA and state policy for having a developmental delay, a diagnosed physical or mental condition, or being at risk for having a substantial delay. If so, your child is generally found to be eligible for services.
- **Initial assessment of the child.** With parental consent, an in-depth assessment must now be conducted to determine your child's unique needs and the early intervention services appropriate to address those needs. Initial

assessment will include reviewing the results of the evaluation, personal observation of your child, and identifying his or her needs in each developmental area.
- **Initial assessment of the family.** With the approval of the family members involved, assessments of family members are also conducted to identify the resources, concerns, and priorities of the family related to enhancing the development of your child. The family-directed assessment is voluntary on the part of each family member participating in the assessment and is based on information gathered through an assessment tool and also through an interview with those family members who elect to participate.
- **Who pays for all this?** Under the IDEA, evaluations and assessments are provided at no cost to parents. They are funded by state and federal monies.

WRITING THE INDIVIDUALIZED FAMILY SERVICE PLAN

Having collected a great deal of information about your child and family, it is now possible for the team (including you as parents) to sit down and write an individualized plan of action for your child and family. This plan is called the "Individualized Family Service Plan" (IFSP). It is a very important document, and you, as parents, are important members of the team that develops it. Each state has specific guidelines for the IFSP. Your service coordinator can explain what the IFSP guidelines are in your state.

- **Guiding principles.** The IFSP is a written document that, among other things, outlines the early intervention services that your child and family will receive. One guiding principle of the IFSP is that the family is a child's greatest resource and that a young child's needs are closely tied to the needs of his or her family. The best way to support children and meet their needs is to support and build upon the individual strengths of their family. So the IFSP is a whole family plan with the parents as major contributors to its development. The involvement of other team members will depend on what the child needs. These other team members could come from several agencies

and may include medical people, therapists, child development specialists, social workers, and others.
- **What info is included in an IFSP?** Your child's IFSP must include the following:
  - your child's present physical, cognitive, communication, social/emotional, and adaptive development levels and needs
  - family information (with your agreement), including the resources, priorities, and concerns of you, as parents, and other family members closely involved with the child
  - the major results or outcomes expected to be achieved for your child and family
  - the specific services your child will be receiving
  - where in the natural environment (e.g., home and community) the services will be provided (If the services will not be provided in the natural environment, the IFSP must include a statement justifying why not.)
  - when and where your son or daughter will receive services
  - the number of days or sessions he or she will receive each service and how long each session will last
  - who will pay for the services
  - the name of the service coordinator overseeing the implementation of the IFSP
  - the steps to be taken to support your child's transition out of early intervention and into another program when the time comes

The IFSP may also identify services your family may be interested in, such as financial information or information about raising a child with a disability.
- **Informed parental consent**. The IFSP must be fully explained to you, the parents, and your suggestions must be considered. You must give written consent for each service to be provided. If you do not give your consent in writing, your child will not receive that service.

- **Reviewing and updating the IFSP.** The IFSP is reviewed every six months and is updated at least once a year. This takes into account that children can learn, grow, and change quickly in just a short period of time.

WHO PAYS FOR THE SERVICES?

Whether or not you, as parents, will have to pay for any services for your child depends on the policies of your state. Check with your service coordinator. Your state's system of payments must be available in writing and given to you, so there are no surprises or unexpected bills later.
- **What is free to families?** Under Part C of the IDEA, the following services must be provided at no cost to families:
  - Child Find services
  - evaluations and assessments
  - the development and review of the IFSP
  - service coordination
- **When services are not free.** Depending on your state's policies, you may have to pay for certain other services. You may be charged a "sliding scale" fee, meaning the fees are based on what you earn. Some services may be covered by your health insurance, Medicaid, or Indian Health Service. The Part C system may ask for your permission to access your public or private insurance in order to pay for the early intervention services your child receives. In most cases, the early intervention system may not use your health care insurance (private or public) without your express, written consent. If you do not give such consent, the system may not limit or deny you or your child services.[1]

---

[1] Center for Parent Information & Resources (CPIR), "Overview of Early Intervention," U.S. Department of Education (ED), July 2021. Available online. URL: www.parentcenterhub.org/ei-overview. Accessed February 9, 2024.

Chapter 17 | Educational Interventions

Learning disabilities have no cure, but early intervention can lessen their effects. People with learning disabilities can develop ways to cope with their disabilities. Getting help earlier increases the chance of success in school and later in life. If learning disabilities remain untreated, a child may begin to feel frustrated, which can lead to low self-esteem and other problems. Experts can help a child learn skills by building on the child's strengths and finding ways to compensate for the child's weaknesses. Interventions vary depending on the nature and extent of the disability.

SPECIAL EDUCATION SERVICES

Children diagnosed with learning disabilities can receive special education services. The Individuals with Disabilities Education Act (IDEA) requires that public schools provide free special education support to children with disabilities. In most states, each child is entitled to these services beginning at the age of three and extending through high school or until the age of 21, whichever comes first. The rules of the IDEA for each state are available from the Early Childhood Technical Assistance Center (ECTAC). The IDEA requires that children be taught in the least restrictive environment appropriate for them. This means the teaching environment should meet a child's needs and skills while minimizing restrictions to typical learning experiences.

INDIVIDUALIZED EDUCATION PROGRAM

Children who qualify for special education services will receive an Individualized Education Program (IEP). This personalized and written education plan:
- lists goals for the child
- specifies the services the child will receive
- lists the specialists who will work with the child

QUALIFYING FOR SPECIAL EDUCATION SERVICES

To qualify for special education services, a child must be evaluated by the school system and meet federal and state guidelines. Parents and caregivers can contact their school principal or special education coordinator to find out how to have their child evaluated. Parents can also review the following resources:
- The Center for Parent Information and Resources (CPIR; www.parentcenterhub.org) offers information about Parent Training and Information Centers (PTIs) and Community Parent Resource Centers (CPRCs; www.parentcenterhub.org/the-parent-center-network)
- IDEA Parent Guide (www.ncld.org/archives/reports-and-studies/idea-parent-guide-2)

INTERVENTIONS FOR SPECIFIC LEARNING DISABILITIES

The following are just a few of the ways schools help children with specific learning disabilities.

Dyslexia
- **Intensive teaching techniques.** These can include specific, step-by-step, and very methodical approaches to teaching reading with the goal of improving both spoken language and written language skills. These techniques are generally more intensive in terms of how often they occur and how long they last and often involve small group or one-on-one instruction.
- **Classroom modifications.** Teachers can give students with dyslexia extra time to finish tasks and provide taped tests that allow the child to hear the questions instead of reading them.

- **Use of technology.** Children with dyslexia may benefit from listening to audiobooks or using word-processing programs.

Dysgraphia

- **Special tools.** Teachers can offer oral exams, provide a notetaker, or allow the child to videotape reports instead of writing them. Computer software can facilitate children being able to produce written text.
- **Use of technology.** A child with dysgraphia can be taught to use word-processing programs, including those incorporating speech-to-text translation, or an audio recorder instead of writing by hand.
- **Reducing the need for writing.** Teachers can provide notes, outlines, and preprinted study sheets.

Dyscalculia

- **Visual techniques.** Teachers can draw pictures of word problems and show the students how to use colored pencils to differentiate parts of problems.
- **Memory aids.** Rhymes and music can help a child remember math concepts.
- **Computers.** A child with dyscalculia can use a computer for drills and practice.[1]

---

[1] "What Are the Treatments for Learning Disabilities?" *Eunice Kennedy Shriver* National Institute of Child Health and Human Development (NICHD), September 11, 2018. Available online. URL: www.nichd.nih.gov/health/topics/learning/conditioninfo/treatment. Accessed February 9, 2024.

Chapter 18 | Special Education Process

Chapter Contents

Section 18.1—Steps in Special Education..............................132

Section 18.2—Individuals with Disabilities Education Act.................136

Section 18.3—Guide to the Individualized Education Program 138

Section 18.1 | Steps in Special Education

When a child is having trouble in school, it is important to find out why. The child may have a disability. By law, schools must provide special help to eligible children with disabilities. This help is called "special education and related services." There is a lot to know about the process by which children are identified as having a disability and in need of special education and related services.

Here, the process has been distilled into 10 basic steps. Once you have the big picture of the process, it is easier to understand the many details under each step.

STEP 1: THE CHILD IS IDENTIFIED AS POSSIBLY NEEDING SPECIAL EDUCATION AND RELATED SERVICES

There are two primary ways in which children are identified as possibly needing special education and related services: the system known as "Child Find" (which operates in each state) and by referral of a parent or school personnel.

- **Child Find.** Each state is required by the Individuals with Disabilities Education Act (IDEA) to identify, locate, and evaluate all children with disabilities in the state who need special education and related services. To do so, states conduct what are known as "Child Find activities." When a child is identified by Child Find as possibly having a disability and needing special education, parents may be asked for permission to evaluate their child. Parents can also call the Child Find office and ask that their child be evaluated.
- **Referral or request for evaluation.** A school professional may ask that a child be evaluated to see if he or she has a disability. Parents may also contact the child's teacher or other school professional to ask that their child be evaluated. This request may be verbal, but it is best to put it in writing.

Parental consent is needed before a child may be evaluated. Under the federal IDEA regulations, evaluation needs to be completed within 60 days after the parent gives consent. However, if a state's IDEA regulations give a different timeline for completion of the evaluation, the state's timeline is applied.

STEP 2: THE CHILD IS EVALUATED
Evaluation is an essential early step in the special education process for a child. It is intended to answer the following questions:
- Does the child have a disability that requires the provision of special education and related services?
- What are the child's specific educational needs?
- What special education services and related services, then, are appropriate for addressing those needs?

By law, the initial evaluation of the child must be "full and individual"—which is to say, focused on that child and that child alone. The evaluation must assess the child in all areas related to the child's suspected disability. The evaluation results will be used to decide the child's eligibility for special education and related services and to make decisions about an appropriate educational program for the child. If the parents disagree with the evaluation, they have the right to take their child for an Independent Educational Evaluation (IEE). They can ask that the school system pay for this IEE.

STEP 3: ELIGIBILITY IS DECIDED
A group of qualified professionals and the parents look at the child's evaluation results. Together, they decide if the child is a "child with a disability," as defined by the IDEA. If the parents do not agree with the eligibility decision, they may ask for a hearing to challenge the decision.

STEP 4: THE CHILD IS FOUND ELIGIBLE FOR SERVICES
If the child is found to be a child with a disability, as defined by the IDEA, he or she is eligible for special education and related services. Within 30 calendar days after a child is determined eligible, a team of school professionals and the parents must meet to write an Individualized Education Program (IEP) for the child.

STEP 5: INDIVIDUALIZED EDUCATION PROGRAM MEETING IS SCHEDULED

The school system schedules and conducts the IEP meeting. School staff must:
- contact the participants, including the parents
- notify parents early enough to make sure they have an opportunity to attend
- schedule the meeting at a time and place agreeable to parents and the school
- tell the parents the purpose, time, and location of the meeting
- tell the parents who will be attending
- tell the parents that they may invite people to the meeting who have knowledge or special expertise about the child

STEP 6: INDIVIDUALIZED EDUCATION PROGRAM MEETING IS HELD AND THE INDIVIDUALIZED EDUCATION PROGRAM IS WRITTEN

The IEP team gathers to talk about the child's needs and write the student's IEP. Parents and the student (when appropriate) are full participating members of the team. If the child's placement (meaning, where the child will receive his or her special education and related services) is decided by a different group, the parents must be part of that group as well. Before the school system may provide special education and related services to the child for the first time, the parents must give consent. The child begins to receive services as soon as possible after the IEP is written and this consent is given.

If the parents do not agree with the IEP and placement, they may discuss their concerns with other members of the IEP team and try to work out an agreement. If they still disagree, parents can ask for Mediation (www.parentcenterhub.org/mediation), or the school may offer mediation. Parents may file a state complaint with the state education agency or a due process complaint, which is the first step in requesting a due process hearing, at which time mediation must be available.

STEP 7: AFTER THE INDIVIDUALIZED EDUCATION PROGRAM IS WRITTEN, SERVICES ARE PROVIDED

The school makes sure that the child's IEP is carried out as it was written. Parents are given a copy of the IEP. Each of the child's teachers and service providers has access to the IEP and knows his or her specific responsibilities for carrying out the IEP. This includes the accommodations, modifications, and support that must be provided to the child in keeping with the IEP.

STEP 8: PROGRESS IS MEASURED AND REPORTED TO PARENTS

The child's progress toward the annual goals is measured, as stated in the IEP. His or her parents are regularly informed of their child's progress and whether that progress is enough for the child to achieve the goals by the end of the year. These progress reports must be given to parents at least as often as parents are informed of their nondisabled children's progress.

STEP 9: INDIVIDUALIZED EDUCATION PROGRAM IS REVIEWED

The child's IEP is reviewed by the IEP team at least once a year or more often if the parents or school ask for a review. If necessary, the IEP is revised. Parents, as team members, must be invited to participate in these meetings. Parents can make suggestions for changes, agree or disagree with the IEP, and agree or disagree with the placement.

If parents do not agree with the IEP and placement, they may discuss their concerns with other members of the IEP team and try to work out an agreement. There are several options, including additional testing, an independent evaluation, or asking for mediation, or a due process hearing. They may also file a complaint with the state education agency.

STEP 10: THE CHILD IS REEVALUATED

At least every three years, the child must be reevaluated. This evaluation is sometimes called a "triennial." Its purpose is to find out if the child continues to be a child with a disability, as defined by the IDEA, and what the child's educational needs are. However, the child must be reevaluated more often if conditions warrant or if the child's parent or teacher asks for a new evaluation.[1]

Section 18.2 | Individuals with Disabilities Education Act

The Individuals with Disabilities Education Act (IDEA) is a law that makes available a free appropriate public education (FAPE) to eligible children with disabilities throughout the nation and ensures special education and related services to those children. The IDEA governs how states and public agencies provide early intervention, special education, and related services to more than 7.5 million (as of school year 2020–2021) eligible infants, toddlers, children, and youth with disabilities. Infants and toddlers, from birth through two years of age, with disabilities and their families receive early intervention services under IDEA Part C. Children and youth aged 3–21 receive special education and related services under IDEA Part B. Additionally, the IDEA authorizes:

- formula grants to states to support special education and related services and early intervention services
- discretionary grants to state educational agencies, institutions of higher education, and other nonprofit organizations to support research, demonstrations, technical assistance and dissemination, technology development, personnel preparation and development, and parent training and information centers

Congress reauthorized the IDEA in 2004 and amended the IDEA through Public Law 114–95, the Every Student Succeeds Act (ESSA), in December 2015. In the law, Congress states:

> Disability is a natural part of the human experience and in no way diminishes the right of individuals to participate

---

[1] Center for Parent Information & Resources (CPIR), "10 Basic Steps in Special Education," U.S. Department of Education (ED), April 2022. Available online. URL: www.parentcenterhub.org/steps. Accessed February 9, 2024.

in or contribute to society. Improving educational results for children with disabilities is an essential element of our national policy of ensuring equality of opportunity, full participation, independent living, and economic self-sufficiency for individuals with disabilities.

INDIVIDUALS WITH DISABILITIES EDUCATION ACT PURPOSE
The stated purpose of the IDEA is:
- to ensure that all children with disabilities have available to them a FAPE that emphasizes special education and related services designed to meet their unique needs and prepare them for further education, employment, and independent living
- to ensure that the rights of children with disabilities and parents of such children are protected
- to assist states, localities, educational service agencies, and federal agencies to provide for the education of all children with disabilities
- to assist states in the implementation of a statewide, comprehensive, coordinated, multidisciplinary, and interagency system of early intervention services for infants and toddlers with disabilities and their families
- to ensure that educators and parents have the necessary tools to improve educational results for children with disabilities by supporting system improvement activities; coordinated research and personnel preparation; coordinated technical assistance, dissemination, and support; and technology development and media services
- to assess, and ensure the effectiveness of, efforts to educate children with disabilities[2]

---

[2] "About IDEA," U.S. Department of Education (ED), December 15, 2015. Available online. URL: https://sites.ed.gov/idea/about-idea. Accessed February 9, 2024.

Section 18.3 | Guide to the Individualized Education Program

WHAT IS AN INDIVIDUALIZED EDUCATION PROGRAM?

An Individualized Education Program (IEP) is a written statement of the educational program designed to meet a child's individual needs. Every child who receives special education services must have an IEP. That is why the process of developing this vital document is of great interest and importance to educators, administrators, and families alike.

Each child's IEP must contain specific information, as listed within the Individuals with Disabilities Education Act (IDEA), our nation's special education law. This includes (but is not limited to):

- the child's present levels of academic achievement and functional performance, describing how the child is currently doing in school and how the child's disability affects his or her involvement and progress in the general curriculum
- annual goals for the child, meaning what parents and the school team think he or she can reasonably accomplish in a year
- the special education and related services to be provided to the child, including supplementary aids and services (such as a communication device) and changes to the program or support for school personnel
- how much of the school day the child will be educated separately from nondisabled children or not participate in extracurricular or other nonacademic activities such as lunch or clubs
- how (and if) the child is to participate in statewide and district-wide assessments, including what modifications to tests the child needs
- when services and modifications will begin, how often they will be provided, where they will be provided, and how long they will last
- how school personnel will measure the child's progress toward the annual goals

WHAT IS THE INDIVIDUALIZED EDUCATION PROGRAM PURPOSE?

The IEP has the following two general purposes:
- to set reasonable learning goals for a child
- to state the services that the school district will provide for the child

WHO DEVELOPS THE INDIVIDUALIZED EDUCATION PROGRAM?

The IEP is developed by a team of individuals that includes key school staff and the child's parents. The team meets, reviews the assessment information available about the child, and designs an educational program to address the child's educational needs that result from his or her disability.

WHEN IS THE INDIVIDUALIZED EDUCATION PROGRAM DEVELOPED?

An IEP meeting must be held within 30 calendar days after it is determined, through a full and individual evaluation, that a child has one of the disabilities listed in the IDEA and needs special education and related services. A child's IEP must also be reviewed at least annually thereafter to determine whether the annual goals are being achieved and must be revised as appropriate.

CAN STUDENTS BE INVOLVED IN DEVELOPING THEIR OWN INDIVIDUALIZED EDUCATION PROGRAM?

The IDEA actually requires that the student be invited to any IEP meeting where transition services will be discussed. These are services designed to help the student plan for his or her transition to adulthood and life after high school.[3]

To write an effective IEP for a child with a disability, parents, teachers, other school staff, and often the child come together at a meeting to look closely at the child's unique needs.

These individuals combine their knowledge, experience, and commitment to design an educational program that must help the child to be involved in, and progress in, the general education

---

[3] Center for Parent Information & Resources (CPIR), "The Short-and-Sweet IEP Overview," U.S. Department of Education (ED), April 2022. Available online. URL: www.parentcenterhub.org/iep-overview. Accessed February 9, 2024.

curriculum—that is, the same curriculum as for children without disabilities. The IEP guides the delivery of special education and related services and supplementary aids and support for the child with a disability. Without a doubt, writing—and implementing—an effective IEP requires teamwork.

Here is a list of IEP team members, as specified in the IDEA, our nation's special education law. Note that the order in which the IEP team members are going to be listed and discussed has nothing to do with their priority on the team. Every member has an equal say and important expertise to contribute.

THE INDIVIDUALIZED EDUCATION PROGRAM TEAM

The IDEA (at §300.321) describes the IEP team as including the following members:
- the parents of the child
- not less than one regular education teacher of the child (if the child is, or maybe, participating in the regular education environment)
- not less than one special education teacher of the child or, where appropriate, not less than one special education provider of the child
- a representative of the public agency who is qualified to provide, or supervise the provision of, specially designed instruction to meet the unique needs of children with disabilities; is knowledgeable about the general education curriculum; and is knowledgeable about the availability of resources of the public agency
- an individual who can interpret the instructional implications of evaluation results
- other individuals who have knowledge or special expertise regarding the child, including related services personnel as appropriate (invited at the discretion of the parent or the agency)
- the child with a disability (when appropriate)[4]

---

[4] Center for Parent Information & Resources (CPIR), "The IEP Team," U.S. Department of Education (ED), April 2022. Available online. URL: www.parentcenterhub.org/iep-team. Accessed February 9, 2024.

THE BIG PICTURE

Before diving into the specifics of what must be included in an IEP, it is important to consider the "Big Picture" of the IEP—its purposes, how it serves as a blueprint for the child's special education and related services under the IDEA, and the scope of activities and settings it covers.

The IEP has the following two general purposes:
- to establish measurable annual goals for the child
- to state the special education and related services and supplementary aids and services that the public agency will provide to, or on behalf of, the child

When constructing an appropriate educational program for a child with a disability, the IEP team broadly considers the child's involvement and participation in the following three main areas of school life:
- the general education curriculum
- extracurricular activities
- nonacademic activities

The general education curriculum refers to the subject matter provided to children without disabilities and the associated skills they are expected to develop and apply. Examples include math, science, history, and language arts.

When the IEP talks about extracurricular activities and nonacademic activities, it is referring to school activities that fall outside the realm of the general curriculum. These are usually voluntary and tend to be more social than academic. They typically involve others of the same age and may be organized and guided by teachers or other school personnel (e.g., yearbook, school newspaper, school sports, school clubs, lunch, recess, band, pep rallies, assemblies, field trips, after-school programs, and recreational clubs).

The IEP can be understood as the blueprint, or plan, for the special education experience of a child with a disability across these school environments.[5]

---

[5] Center for Parent Information & Resources (CPIR), "Contents of the IEP," U.S. Department of Education (ED), April 2022. Available online. URL: www.parentcenterhub.org/iepcontents. Accessed February 9, 2024.

Chapter 19 | Support and Accommodations for Students

SUPPORT TYPES
For many students with disabilities—and for many without—the key to success in the classroom lies in having appropriate adaptations, accommodations, and modifications made to the instruction and other classroom activities. Some adaptations are as simple as moving a distractible student to the front of the class or away from the pencil sharpener or the window. Other modifications may involve changing the way that material is presented or the way that students respond to show their learning.

Adaptations, accommodations, and modifications need to be individualized for students, based on their needs and their personal learning styles and interests. It is not always obvious what adaptations, accommodations, or modifications would be beneficial for a particular student, or how changes to the curriculum, its presentation, the classroom setting, or student evaluation might be made.

DIFFERENT TYPES OF SUPPORT
Special Education
By definition, special education is "specially designed instruction" (§300.39). And, the Individuals with Disabilities Education Act (IDEA) defines that term as follows:

> Specially designed instruction means adapting, as appropriate to the needs of an eligible child under this part, the content, methodology, or delivery of instruction—(i) To address the unique needs of the child that result from the

child's disability; and (ii) To ensure access of the child to the general curriculum, so that the child can meet the educational standards within the jurisdiction of the public agency that apply to all children. (§300.39(b)(3)).

Thus, special education involves adapting the "content, methodology, or delivery of instruction."

Adapting Instruction

Sometimes a student may need to have changes made in classwork or routines because of his or her disability. Modifications can be made to:
- what a child is taught
- how a child works at school

Modifications or accommodations are most often made in the following areas:
- **Scheduling**:
  - giving the student extra time to complete assignments or tests
  - breaking up testing over several days
- **Setting**:
  - working in a small group
  - working one-on-one with the teacher
- **Materials**:
  - providing audiotaped lectures or books
  - giving copies of the teacher's lecture notes
  - using large print books, Braille, or books on compact disc (CD; digital text)
- **Instruction**:
  - reducing the difficulty of assignments
  - reducing the reading level
  - using a student/peer tutor
- **Student response**:
  - allowing answers to be given orally or dictated
  - using a word processor for written work
  - using sign language, a communication device, Braille, or a native language if it is not English

Because adapting the content, methodology, and/or delivery of instruction is an essential element in special education and an extremely valuable support for students, it is equally essential to know as much as possible about how instruction can be adapted to address the needs of an individual student with a disability. The special education teacher who serves on the Individualized Education Program (IEP) team can contribute his or her expertise in this area, which is the essence of special education.

Related Services

It is clear from the IDEA's definition of related services at §300.34 that these services are supportive in nature, although not in the same way that adapting the curriculum is. Related services support children's special education and are provided when necessary to help students benefit from special education. That definition begins: §300.34 Related Services.

(a) General. Related services means transportation and such developmental, corrective, and other supportive services as are required to assist a child with a disability to benefit from special education.

Here is the list of related services in the law:
- speech-language pathology and audiology services
- interpreting services
- psychological services
- physical and occupational therapy
- recreation, including therapeutic recreation
- early identification and assessment of disabilities in children
- counseling services, including rehabilitation counseling
- orientation and mobility services
- medical services for diagnostic or evaluation purposes
- school health services and school nurse services
- social work services in schools

Supplementary Aids and Services

One of the most powerful types of support available to children with disabilities is the other kinds of support or services (other than special education and related services) that a child needs to be educated with nondisabled children to the maximum extent appropriate. Some examples of these additional services and support, called "supplementary aids and services" in the IDEA, are:

- adapted equipment—such as a special seat or a cutout cup for drinking
- assistive technology—such as a word processor, special software, or a communication system
- training for staff, students, and/or parents
- peer tutors
- a one-on-one aid
- adapted materials—such as books on tape, large print, or highlighted notes
- collaboration/consultation among staff, parents, and/or other professionals

The IEP team, which includes the parents, is the group that decides which supplementary aids and services a child needs to support his or her access to and participation in the school environment. The IEP team must really work together to make sure that a child gets the supplementary aids and services that he or she needs to be successful. Team members talk about the child's needs, curriculum, and school routine and openly explore all options to make sure the right support for the specific child is included.[1]

ACCOMMODATIONS IN POSTSECONDARY EDUCATION INSTITUTIONS

Postsecondary education institutions are not required to provide a free and appropriate public education (FAPE), as the high school was. Under the Americans with Disabilities Act (ADA) and Section 504, postsecondary schools are only required to provide "reasonable and appropriate accommodations, academic adjustments, and/or auxiliary aids" as needed to ensure that it does not discriminate on the basis of disability. As adults, students

---

[1] Center for Parent Information & Resources (CPIR), "Supports, Modifications, and Accommodations for Students," U.S. Department of Education (ED), March 2022. Available online. URL: www.parentcenterhub.org/accommodations/#part2. Accessed February 8, 2024.

Support and Accommodations for Students | 147

are required to advocate for their own accommodations. Parents may or may not be allowed to participate in arranging student accommodations.

Most postsecondary schools have disability services offices, which may help with arranging and documenting the accommodations needed and requested by students, but the postsecondary education institution is not required to assist a student with self-advocacy. Some disability services offices will allow parents to participate if the student signs a privacy waiver allowing them to share the student's private information. In order to obtain these accommodations, students are required to provide documentation showing they have a current disability and need an academic adjustment. If the postsecondary school requires a new evaluation, the student may be required to pay for it. However, if the student is eligible for vocational rehabilitation (VR) services, the VR agency may cover the cost of the new evaluations under the Individualized Plan for Employment (IPE).

It is also important to understand that the postsecondary school is not required to lower or substantially modify essential academic requirements. It is not required to change the substantive content of the course curriculum or tests as the secondary school was. Available postsecondary school accommodations are individualized and vary, but some common accommodations include the following:

- extended time on exams (not the same as "untimed" tests, which are not typically available)
- use of laptops for tests and exams
- use of calculators for tests and exams
- permission to make audio recordings of classes (Some schools may loan out smart pens for this purpose.)
- reduced course load (note that financial aid may be reduced as a result)
- priority registration for courses
- copies of notes from a classmate
- access to audiobooks
- access to voice recognition software
- access to text-to-speech programs

Postsecondary schools are also required to provide "auxiliary aids" as part of their responsibilities to make their programs accessible. Some of these might be considered assistive technology devices and services. Examples include the following:

- digital audio texts
- notetakers
- interpreters
- readers
- talking calculators
- electronic readers
- Braille calculators, printers, or typewriters
- telephone handset amplifiers
- closed caption decoders
- open and closed video captioning
- voice synthesizers
- calculators or keyboards with large buttons
- reaching device for library use
- assistive listening devices

If an auxiliary aid is necessary for the classroom or other appropriate (nonpersonal) use, the postsecondary school must make it available, unless the provision of the aid would cause undue burden as defined under the ADA. A postsecondary student with a disability may not be required to pay part or all of the costs of that auxiliary aid or service. If the cost of the auxiliary aid or service is considered an undue burden, the postsecondary student may try to obtain reimbursement for the cost of aid from the state VR agency.[2]

---

[2] Center for Parent Information & Resources (CPIR), "Young Adults in Transition: Vocational Rehabilitation Services: Part 5," U.S. Department of Education (ED), January 20, 2020. Available online. URL: www.parentcenterhub.org/young-adults-in-transition-vr-services-5. Accessed February 8, 2024.

Chapter 20 | Preemployment Transition Services

Chapter Contents
Section 20.1—Vocational Rehabilitation Services..................150
Section 20.2—Individualized Plan for Employment..................158

Section 20.1 | Vocational Rehabilitation Services

The Individuals with Disabilities Education Act (IDEA) requires planning for the transition from school to adult life for students with disabilities to begin at the age of 16. Many states begin earlier, at around the age of 14. In addition to prevocational education and work experiences provided by the school, students should prepare for receiving vocational rehabilitation (VR) services from their state's VR agency if they expect to be eligible for these services. VR agencies, which are found in every state, offer VR services to eligible persons with disabilities to help them prepare for, retain, regain, or advance in employment. Some states have separate VR agencies serving individuals who are visually impaired or with communication disability. VR agencies are also required to provide a specific set of services for secondary students who may not be presumed to be—or ever be deemed—eligible for general VR services called "Pre-Employment Transition Services" (Pre-ETS).

ABOUT VOCATIONAL REHABILITATION AGENCIES

Vocational rehabilitation agencies were created by the Rehabilitation Act of 1973 (Rehab Act). Under Title I of the Rehab Act, states receive money to provide VR services to persons with disabilities. VR agencies use this money to fund a wide range of goods and services that are connected to a person's vocational goal. Eligible individuals have a right to these services under federal and state laws. The Rehab Act is based on the principle that "people with disabilities are capable of achieving high quality, competitive and integrated employment (CIE) when provided the necessary services and supports." State-run VR systems were created to provide the services persons with disabilities need in order to participate in job-driven training and to pursue high-quality employment outcomes.

Since 1986, the Rehab Act has required VR agencies to "maximize the employment" outcome for those receiving VR services. This change expanded VR services to increase the potential of individuals with disabilities to achieve CIE. Nowadays, the law continues to reinforce and ensure its original intent: "Individuals with disabilities, with appropriate supports and services, are able to achieve the same kinds of CIE as nondisabled individuals." It also now places a greater emphasis on serving people with disabilities, including people with the most significant disabilities, and VR agencies' responsibility to help them achieve CIE in an integrated setting.

ELIGIBILITY FOR VOCATIONAL REHABILITATION SERVICES
To be eligible for VR services, the individual must:
- have a physical, mental, emotional, or learning disability that is a real barrier to the individual getting and keeping a job
- need VR services to prepare the individual to get, keep, or regain employment
- be able to benefit from the services that will help the individual get and keep the job or to benefit from independent living

If the individual receives Supplemental Security Income (SSI) and/or Social Security Disability Insurance (SSDI), they are automatically considered eligible. But it is important to note that the individual does not need to be eligible for or receiving SSI or SSDI in order to be eligible for VR services. Students who are in special education programs, receive accommodations in school, or have severe health conditions may be eligible. Applicants for VR services must have a "substantial impediment"—a mental, physical, or learning disability—that interferes with their ability to work and hinders their access to an ultimate employment goal. The regulations indicate that "impediment" should be interpreted broadly.

A substantial impediment must also cause a person to need VR services in order to "prepare for, secure, retain, advance in, or regain employment," and the applicant must be able to benefit from VR services. Before a VR agency can determine that an individual cannot benefit from VR services, it must explore the individual's work potential through a variety of assessments and trial work experiences. Examples might include supported employment

or on-the-job training in realistic work situations. The trial work experiences must:
- be in CIE settings to the maximum extent appropriate
- be of sufficient variety and over a sufficient length of time to determine whether the individual can benefit from services
- provide support (such as assistive technology and personal assistance services (PAS))

In order to decide that a person cannot benefit from VR services, the VR agency must show "clear and convincing" evidence that they cannot benefit through the provision of support. "Clear and convincing evidence" must include a functional assessment of skills with any necessary support (including assistive technology) in real-life settings. An additional set of school-to-work transition services called "Pre-ETS" are provided by VR agencies to students with disabilities while they are still in secondary school. Pre-ETS do not require a VR eligibility determination.

ORDER OF SELECTION

Not all individuals who are eligible will necessarily receive VR services. VR agencies are required to serve individuals with the most significant disabilities first when there are not enough resources to serve everyone who is eligible. This means that "individuals with the most significant disabilities" are given priority over those with less significant disabilities. This process is called an "order of selection" (OOS). The federal regulations do not specifically define "individual with a most significant disability." State VR agencies are given discretion in how they define an individual with a most significant disability. Typically, the categories they define will consider:
- the number of functional capacities affected
- the need for multiple VR services for an extended period of time
- the existence of one or more physical or mental disabilities

VOCATIONAL REHABILITATION EVALUATIONS AND ASSESSMENTS

Vocational assessment is the process of determining an individual's interests, abilities, aptitudes, and skills to identify vocational strengths, needs, and career potential. Vocational assessment may use a variety of standardized techniques (tests) or nonstandardized approaches (interviews, observing people). For students transitioning from secondary school, VR agencies may also review evaluations and other documents from the student's school years.

Parents and school districts should consider updating assessments in anticipation of the student's referral to the VR agency. However, the VR agency is ultimately responsible for obtaining any additional assessments that it needs to determine eligibility for VR services. VR agencies sometimes perform "situational assessments," to assess work behaviors, work tolerance, ability to follow instructions, work with others, and more. These involve placing the person in an actual work situation to assess their performance. Such assessments can also be used to assess job-specific work skills and abilities. If a student of transition age has had work experience during their school years, documentation from the student's performance in these settings may also be considered.[1]

SPECIAL EDUCATION TRANSITION AND VOCATIONAL REHABILITATION SERVICES

Understanding VR services is particularly important to students and their families during the transition from school to adult life. State VR agencies are required to respond to requests from the school district to collaborate on transition planning. Having VR representatives at the Individualized Education Plan (IEP) table and developing positive working relationships with VR while a student is still in school can help smooth the transition between these two service systems.

---

[1] Center for Parent Information & Resources (CPIR), "Young Adults in Transition: Vocational Rehabilitation Services: Part 1," U.S. Department of Education (ED), December 3, 2019. Available online. URL: www.parentcenterhub.org/young-adults-in-transition-vr-services-1. Accessed February 8, 2024.

How Do Families and Youth Involve the State Vocational Rehabilitation Agency in Transition Planning?

School personnel—including but not limited to special educators, guidance counselors, school nurses, school psychologists, speech/language pathologists, administrators, and general education teachers, as well as parents/guardians—may refer students to VR and request that they participate in planning during the student's secondary school years.

Students may be referred for VR services at the earliest age established by the state VR agency, and there is no minimum age given in the statute. In general, the VR system recommends that students who are expected to be eligible for VR services be referred and apply at least two years before leaving school. For students who are involved in or expect to be involved in Community-Based Work Experiences (CBWEs), referral and application are generally recommended at the age of 16 but may begin earlier. Many states begin with a referral at the age of 14.

If a Student Is Presumed or Expected to Be Eligible for Vocational Rehabilitation Services

VR agencies can help students with disabilities transition from school into postsecondary education, into training, or directly into employment with the ultimate goal of meaningful inclusion in the adult community. The VR Transition Counselor may work with school staff to provide assistance with transition planning, developing postsecondary goals, developing appropriate VR referrals, or educating school staff, parents, students, and others about available VR programs. Once VR refers someone, they may also help students get an early start on the application and VR services eligibility determination process.

Once a student is determined eligible for VR services, the student or their representative develops an individualized plan for VR services called the "Individualized Plan for Employment" (IPE). The student or their representative may seek assistance in the development of the IPE from family members, a knowledgeable advocate, or other individuals. However, only a qualified VR Counselor employed by the VR agency may approve and sign the IPE.

If a Student Is Not Presumed or Expected to Be Eligible for Vocational Rehabilitation Services

The VR agency must provide services for students who may not be eligible for VR services while they are still in secondary school. VR agencies are now required to use 15 percent of their public VR funding on a specific set of services for secondary students called "Pre-ETS." Students are not required to be determined eligible for VR services or have developed an IPE in order to receive these services. There are five required Pre-ETS that VR can provide to students with disabilities while they are still students:

- job exploration counseling
- work-based learning experiences, which may include in-school or after-school opportunities or experiences outside the traditional school setting
- counseling on opportunities for enrollment in comprehensive transition or postsecondary educational programs at institutions of higher education
- workplace readiness training to develop social skills and independent living
- instruction in self-advocacy, which may include peer mentoring[2]

REQUIRED VOCATIONAL REHABILITATION SERVICES

Vocational rehabilitation services are any services, described in an IPE, necessary to assist a person with a disability in "preparing for, securing, retaining, advancing in, or regaining an employment outcome that is consistent with the strengths, resources, priorities, concerns, abilities, capabilities, interests, and informed choice of the individual." Even if a state limits VR services by going to an OOS, the VR agency must serve each applicant for services who are in a category that is eligible to be served, and it must provide all needed services to each individual it serves. The services that are available from the VR system are incredibly broad and varied.

---

[2] Center for Parent Information & Resources (CPIR), "Young Adults in Transition: Vocational Rehabilitation Services: Part 2," U.S. Department of Education (ED), March 18, 2020. Available online. URL: www.parentcenterhub.org/young-adults-in-transition-vr-services-2. Accessed February 8, 2024.

Essentially, whatever an individual with a disability needs to overcome his or her barrier to employment can be covered. VR services must include, but are not limited to, the following:
- the assessment to determine eligibility and needs (if appropriate, conducted by someone skilled in rehabilitation or assistive technology)
- counseling, guidance, and job placement services and, if appropriate, referrals to the services of other agencies, including others within the statewide workforce development system
- vocational and other training, including higher education and the purchase of tools, materials, and books, which includes the following:
  - graduate-level training in any field
  - "Tuition and other services for students with intellectual or developmental disabilities in a Comprehensive Transition and Postsecondary Program for Students with Intellectual Disabilities (TPSID), as defined by the Higher Education Act of 2008."
- diagnosis and treatment of physical or mental impairments to reduce or eliminate impediments to employment, to the extent financial support is not available from other sources, including health insurance or other comparable benefits
- maintenance for additional costs incurred during rehabilitation
- transportation, defined as "travel and related expenses that are necessary to enable an applicant or eligible individual to participate in a VR service" (Additionally, "the purchase and repair of vehicles, including vans" is an example of an expense that would meet the definition of transportation.)
- PAS while receiving VR services
- interpreter services for individuals who are deaf (For individuals who are visually impaired, readers, rehabilitation teaching, and orientation and mobility services can be provided.)

Preemployment Transition Services | 157

- occupational licenses, tools, equipment, initial stocks, and supplies
- technical assistance for those who are pursuing telecommuting, self-employment, or small business operations
- rehabilitation technology (i.e., assistive technology), including vehicular modification, telecommunications, sensory and other technological aids, and other technological aids and devices
- transition services for students with disabilities to facilitate the achievement of the employment outcome identified in the IPE
- supported employment
- customized employment
- services to the family to assist an individual with a disability to achieve an employment outcome
- other goods and services determined necessary to enable the individual with a disability to achieve an employment outcome
- postemployment services necessary to assist an individual to maintain, regain, or advance in employment

VR agencies may also provide services to employers who have hired or are interested in hiring individuals with disabilities, including:
- providing training and technical assistance to employers regarding the employment of individuals with disabilities, including disability awareness, and the requirements of the Americans with Disabilities Act (ADA) of 1990 (42 U.S.C. 12101 et seq.) and other employment-related laws
- working with employers to:
  - provide opportunities for work-based learning experiences (including internships, short-term employment, apprenticeships, and fellowships)
  - provide opportunities for Pre-ETS in accordance with the requirements under 34 C.F.R. 361.48(a)
  - recruit qualified applicants who are individuals with disabilities

- understand how to train employees who are individuals with disabilities
- promote awareness of disability-related obstacles to continued employment
- providing consultation, technical assistance, and support to employers on workplace accommodations, assistive technology, and facilities and workplace access through collaboration with community partners and employers, across states and nationally, to enable the employers to recruit, job match, hire, and retain qualified individuals with disabilities who are recipients of VR under this part or who are applicants for such services
- assisting employers with utilizing available financial support for hiring or accommodating individuals with disabilities[3]

Section 20.2 | Individualized Plan for Employment

After eligibility for vocational rehabilitation (VR) services is established and assessments have been performed, the next step is to develop a written plan to determine the person's employment goal and the specific VR services needed to help the individual reach that goal. This plan is known as the "Individualized Plan for Employment" (IPE). It is developed by the VR "client," with or without assistance from the VR counselor, and is completed on a form provided by the state VR agency. The IPE must be developed no later than 90 days after the person's eligibility determination is made. If necessary, the VR agency and client can agree to an extension to a specified later date.

---

[3] Center for Parent Information & Resources (CPIR), "Young Adults in Transition: Vocational Rehabilitation Services: Part 4," U.S. Department of Education (ED), December 11, 2019. Available online. URL: www.parentcenterhub.org/young-adults-in-transition-vr-services-4. Accessed February 8, 2024.

Preemployment Transition Services | 159

For young adults in school, some of this planning may already have begun. No later than the Individual Educational Program (IEP) year in which the student turns 16, the IEP is required to include postsecondary goals for employment, education/training, and, if appropriate, independent living with specific transition services to assist the student in meeting these goals. Note that in order to include these goals, the IEP must be developed during the prior school year when the student is 15 years old. Understanding the requirements of the VR IPE while in school can help better prepare the student for receiving VR services. The IPE developed while the student is in school must be consistent with the goals in the IEP. For VR services, the IPE must include the following:

- a description of the specific employment outcome chosen by the eligible person that is consistent with the individual's unique strengths, resources, priorities, concerns, abilities, capabilities, career interests, and informed choice
- a description of the specific rehabilitation services that are needed to achieve the employment outcome, including, as appropriate, the provision of assistive technology devices or services and personal assistance services, including training in the management of these services (Services must be provided in the most integrated setting that is appropriate for the services involved and is consistent with the informed choice of the person.)
- timelines for the achievement of the employment outcome and for initiation of services
- a description of the entity or entities chosen by the person (or representative) that will provide the VR services and the methods used to procure these services
- a description of the criteria that will be used to evaluate progress toward achievement of the employment outcome
- the terms and conditions of the IPE, including the rights and responsibilities of the VR agency and the person, the extent of the person's financial participation in paying for the cost of services, the responsibility of the person regarding applying for and securing comparable benefits, and the responsibility of other entities

The IPE must be reviewed at least annually and must be amended if necessary due to changes in employment outcome, VR services to be provided, and VR service providers. Changes made when the IPE is reviewed cannot take place until they are agreed upon by the person and their VR counselor.

EMPLOYMENT GOALS AND OUTCOMES

Employment goals and outcomes are central to the IPE and are defined by law as "entering, advancing in, or retaining full-time or part-time competitive integrated employment (CIE)." They include "customized employment, self-employment, telecommuting, or business ownership."

- CIE is full- or part-time work at minimum wage or higher with wages and benefits similar to those without disabilities performing the same work and fully integrated with coworkers without disabilities.
- Customized employment is CIE for an individual with a significant disability based on a personalized determination of the individual's "strengths, needs, and interests." It is designed to meet the specific abilities of the individual and the business needs of the employer and is carried out with "flexible strategies."
- Supported employment may be a goal for persons with the most significant disabilities who need intensive support and extended services when it is consistent with their unique strengths, priorities, concerns, abilities, capabilities, and interests. Supported employment services can include supplementary assessments of rehabilitation needs, skilled job trainers for the person at the worksite, social skills training, follow-up services, and facilitation of natural support at the worksite. These services are usually provided on a short-term basis when they are expected to lead to competitive employment within two years.
- Telecommuting involves performing job-related functions at a location other than the employer's physical location. Telecommuting can be arranged with some employers for some jobs and performed for part or all of the employee's

work time. VR services can help with expenses related to telecommuting, such as computers, Internet service provider costs, and needed assistive technology devices and services. Telecommuting may be an important IPE goal for persons living in remote rural locations or who may not have access to effective transportation services.
- Business ownership is just that developing and starting one's own business. Although state VR agencies vary in their approaches to funding self-employment, most will require a self-employment feasibility study and/or draft business plan. The funding VR will agree to cover varies as well, and VR agencies may encourage the individual to explore other funding sources and services, such as their local workforce (one-stop) system.

MAXIMIZATION OF EMPLOYMENT

In 1986, the Rehabilitation Act of 1973 was amended to include its purpose to "Empower individuals with disabilities to maximize employment, economic self-sufficiency, independence, and inclusion and integration into society, through comprehensive and coordinated state-of-the-art programs of VR."

In 1992, specific language was included to add, "The purpose of the VR Program is, in part, to empower individuals with disabilities to maximize employment, economic self-sufficiency, independence, and inclusion and integration into society."

Taken together, these amendments are broadly interpreted to mean that if a person has the required ability, the VR agency should provide services to persons who need help to qualify for, find, or keep a job that is consistent with their strengths, resources, priorities, concerns, abilities, interests, and informed choice.

Informed Choice

VR agencies are required to implement their programs and provide information and services with "respect for individual dignity, personal responsibility, self-determination, and pursuit of meaningful careers, based on informed choice, of individuals with disabilities."

This principle and many rules surrounding VR help ensure that the VR process is consumer-driven and that the VR agency's policies and methods facilitate the flexible provision of services and afford eligible persons meaningful choices and services.[4]

---

[4] Center for Parent Information & Resources (CPIR), "Young Adults in Transition: Vocational Rehabilitation Services: Part 3," U.S. Department of Education (ED), January 20, 2020. Available online. URL: www.parentcenterhub.org/young-adults-in-transition-vr-services-3. Accessed February 8, 2024.

Chapter 21 | Transition Planning and Programs

Chapter Contents
Section 21.1—Education and Training Opportunities in High School and
  Secondary School 164
Section 21.2—Planning for Out-of-School Youth......................... 171

Section 21.1 | Education and Training Opportunities in High School and Secondary School

As a student approaches the time to leave high school, it is important that preparations for adult life are well underway. For early transition planning and active participation in decision-making to occur for students with disabilities, members of the planning team need to be well-informed about the student's abilities, needs, and available services. This section highlights educational opportunities, credentials, and employment strategies designed to assist students with disabilities while in school to prepare for a meaningful postsecondary education and/or thriving career.

HIGH SCHOOL EDUCATION AND TRAINING OPPORTUNITIES

There are a number of opportunities and programs available for students preparing to exit secondary school. Many of these education and training opportunities involve formal or informal connections between educational, vocational rehabilitation (VR), employment, training, social services, and health services agencies. Specifically, high schools, career centers, community colleges, four-year colleges and universities, and state technical colleges are key partners. These partners offer federal, state, and local funds to assist students preparing for postsecondary education.

Further, research suggests that enrollment in more rigorous, academically intense programs (e.g., advanced placement, international baccalaureate, or dual enrollment) in high school prepares students, including those with low achievement levels, to enroll and persist in postsecondary education at higher rates than similar students who pursue less challenging courses of study. The following are examples of existing options, programs, and activities that may be available as Individualized Education Program (IEP) teams develop IEPs to prepare the student for the transition to adult life.

Regular High School Diploma

The term "regular high school diploma" means the standard high school diploma awarded to the preponderance of students in the state that is fully aligned with state standards, or a higher diploma, except that a regular high school diploma shall not be aligned to the alternate academic achievement standards. It does not include a recognized equivalent of a diploma, such as a general equivalency diploma, certificate of completion, certificate of attendance, or similar lesser credential.

The vast majority of students with disabilities should have access to the same high-quality academic coursework as all other students in the state that reflects grade-level content for the grade in which the student is enrolled and that enables them to participate in assessments aligned with grade-level achievement standards.

Alternate High School Diploma

Some students with the most significant cognitive disabilities may be awarded a state-defined alternate high school diploma based on alternate academic achievement standards, but that diploma must be standards-based. Working toward an alternate diploma sometimes causes delay or keeps the student from completing the requirements for a regular high school diploma. However, students with the most significant cognitive disabilities who are working toward an alternate diploma must receive instruction that is aligned with the state's challenging academic content standards and that promotes their involvement and progress in the general education curriculum, consistent with the Individuals with Disabilities Education Act (IDEA).

Further, states must continue to make a free appropriate public education (FAPE) available to any student with a disability who graduates from high school with a credential other than a regular high school diploma, such as an alternate diploma, general educational development (GED), or certificate of completion. While FAPE under the IDEA does not include education beyond grade 12, states and school districts are required to continue to offer to develop and implement an IEP for an eligible student with a disability who graduates from high school with a credential other than a regular high school diploma until the student has exceeded the age of eligibility for FAPE under state law.

The IEP for students with disabilities could include transition services in the form of coursework at a community college or other postsecondary institution, provided that the state recognizes the coursework as secondary school education under state law. Secondary school education does not include education that is beyond grade 12 and must meet state education standards.

POSTSECONDARY EDUCATION AND TRAINING OPTIONS
Preparing for College
Secondary School
Whether in middle or high school, if a student eligible for the IDEA is planning to attend college, there are a number of critical steps to be taken to become college-ready. Early in the transition process, a student is encouraged to:

- take interesting and challenging courses that prepare him or her for college
- be involved in school or community-based activities that allow him or her to explore career interests, including work-based learning or internship opportunities
- meet with school guidance counselors to discuss career goals, such as vocational and educational goals, programs of study, and college requirements, including the admissions process and any standardized tests required for admission
- be an active participant during the individualized IEP meetings

As noted earlier, the IEP team is responsible for ensuring that the student's IEP includes the specialized instruction, support, and services needed to assist the student in preparing for college and/or other postsecondary schools. Students with disabilities and their families interested in higher education are encouraged to consider the college environment that provides the best educational program and support services to assist students with meeting their needs and career goals.

IDEA-eligible students with disabilities will benefit from discussions with their parents, school guidance counselor, VR counselor (if applicable), and other professional support staff about the services and support needed to be successful in postsecondary education or training. For IDEA-eligible students whose eligibility terminates because the student has graduated from secondary school with a regular high school diploma or the student has exceeded the age of eligibility for FAPE under state law, the school district must provide the student with a summary of performance that documents the student's academic achievement, functional performance, and recommendations on how to assist the student in meeting his or her postsecondary goals.

Paying for College

The Office of Federal Student Aid (FSA) in the U.S. Department of Education (ED) plays a central role in the nation's postsecondary education community. Through the FSA, the ED awards about $150 billion a year in grants, work-study funds, and low-interest loans to approximately 13 million students. There are three types of federal student aid:

- **Grants and scholarships.** Financial aid that does not have to be repaid, including the Federal Pell Grant that can award as much as $6,345 to each low-income student per year.
- **Work-study.** A program that allows students to earn money for their education.
- **Low-interest loans.** Aid that allows students to borrow money for their education; loans must be repaid with interest.

Completing the Free Application for Federal Student Aid (FAFSA®) is the first step toward getting financial aid for college. The FAFSA® not only provides access to the $150 billion in grants, loans, and work-study funds that the federal government has available, but many states, schools, and private scholarships require students to submit the FAFSA® before they will consider offering any financial aid. That is why it is important that every college-bound student complete the FAFSA®.

Students who participate in comprehensive transition programs are also eligible for federal student financial aid. Students enrolled in a comprehensive transition and postsecondary program for students with intellectual disabilities who are maintaining satisfactory academic progress in that program may receive federal student financial aid under the Federal Pell Grant, Federal Supplemental Educational Opportunity Grant (FSEOG), or Federal Work-Study (FWS) programs.

Choosing the Right College

College is a big investment in time, money, and effort. Therefore, it is important to research and understand the types of schools, tuition and costs, programs available, student enrollment, and a variety of other important factors when choosing the right school. When researching potential college programs, students and their families are advised to work closely with the Disability Support Services (DSS) office on campus to discuss disability-related concerns and needs and the disability-related support services available to students at that postsecondary school. Many DSS offices empower, support, and advocate for students with disabilities to achieve their goals by providing access to education and other programs through the coordination of appropriate accommodations and academic adjustments, assistive technology, alternative formats, and other support. These support and services, including academic adjustments and auxiliary aids, are provided in compliance with Section 504 and the Americans with Disabilities Act (ADA). Title II of the ADA applies to public postsecondary institutions, and Title III of the ADA applies to certain private postsecondary institutions.

EMPLOYMENT OPPORTUNITIES IN THE SECONDARY SCHOOL SETTING

The following list describes work-based strategies used to enhance competitive integrated employment (CIE) opportunities for students and youth with disabilities.

Internships

Internships are formal agreements whereby a student or youth is assigned specific tasks in a workplace over a predetermined period of time. Internships can be paid or unpaid, depending on the nature of the agreement with the company and the nature of the tasks. Internships are usually temporary on-the-job work experiences. They not only provide individuals, including students and youth with disabilities, actual work experience and the opportunity to develop skills but also provide the opportunity to determine if the type of work involved is in keeping with the individuals' career interests, abilities, and goals. There is no guarantee that an internship will lead to a permanent employment offer. However, VR counselors refer students or youth with a disability to an internship to increase their employment opportunities. The internship experience is frequently enriched by the provision of services or support, such as transportation and vocational counseling, as described in an approved Individualized Plan for Employment (IPE) under the VR program.

Mentorships

A young person with or without a disability may participate in a mentoring relationship to hone his or her occupational skills and work habits. The business community describes mentoring as an employee training system under which a senior or more experienced individual (the mentor) is assigned as an advisor, counselor, or guide to a junior or trainee (mentee). The mentor is responsible for providing support to, and feedback on, the individual in his or her charge. The mentor's area of experience is sought based on his or her career, disability, and history or life experience similar to the mentee or a host of other possibilities.

Many schools or existing community organizations, such as the Young Men's Christian Association (YMCA), Boys and Girls Clubs, and Centers for Independent Living, introduce students and youth to older peer or adult mentors who have achieved success in a particular area that is important for the student and youth (e.g., employers, college students, and recovering substance abusers). Interaction with successful role models with disabilities enhances the disability-related knowledge and self-confidence of students and youth with disabilities, as well as parents' perceptions of the knowledge and capabilities of their students and youth with disabilities.

Apprenticeships

Apprenticeships are formal, sanctioned work experiences of extended duration in which an apprentice, frequently known as a "trainee," learns specific occupational skills related to a standardized trade, such as carpentry, plumbing, or drafting. Many apprenticeships also include paid work components. In an apprenticeship program, an individual has the opportunity to learn a trade through on-the-job training as well as through related academic knowledge. Often, these programs involve an employer and a community college or university and a trade union. An individual applies for specific training and, once accepted, is able to participate in the apprenticeship program. Employment opportunities are usually offered to an individual who successfully completes the program. VR counselors assist individuals with disabilities to prepare for the apprenticeship application process, develop a plan to gain the prerequisite knowledge and skills for the trade, and identify support services needed to be successful in the apprenticeship program.

Paid Employment

Paid employment involves existing standard jobs in a company or customized employment positions that are negotiated with an employer. These jobs always feature a wage paid directly to the student or youth. Such work is scheduled during or after the school day. Paid employment is frequently an integral part of a student's course of study or simply a separate adjunctive experience.

Oftentimes, these employment experiences are the first steps toward building a meaningful career for students and youth with disabilities.[1]

---

[1] "A Transition Guide to Postsecondary Education and Employment for Students and Youth with Disabilities," U.S. Department of Education (ED), August 24, 2020. Available online. URL: https://sites.ed.gov/idea/files/postsecondary-transition-guide-august-2020.pdf. Accessed February 8, 2024.

Section 21.2 | Planning for Out-of-School Youth

Transition planning is critical for any youth with a disability, whether they are in school or not. A vocational rehabilitation (VR) counselor can assist youth with disabilities in exploring careers, identifying a career path leading to their vocational goal, and identifying the services and steps to reach that goal. With the exception of preemployment transition services and transition services provided to groups of individuals with disabilities, VR services are provided only to those individuals with disabilities, including youth with disabilities, who have been determined eligible for services, and the services are described in an approved Individualized Plan for Employment (IPE).

Although youth with disabilities who do not meet the definition of a "student with a disability" may not receive preemployment transition services, they may receive transition services as group transition services, prior to or after applying for VR services, as well as individualized transition or other VR services, after being determined eligible for the VR program and under an approved IPE. Individualized transition services provided under an approved IPE to a youth with a disability eligible for the VR program may consist of, among other things, job exploration counseling, including assessments and vocational guidance and counseling; work adjustment training, vocational/occupational training, or postsecondary education; and job development services, including job search, job placement, and job coaching services.

COORDINATION OF SERVICES

The vocational rehabilitation program is designed to assess, plan, develop, and provide VR services to eligible individuals with disabilities, consistent with their strengths, resources, priorities, concerns, abilities, capabilities, interests, and informed choices. The VR agency assigns a VR counselor to each eligible individual, and the VR counselor can help the youth develop the IPE.

A VR counselor can assist youth in finding and applying for essential daily living services and resources, such as health and housing referrals needed to successfully implement their employment plans.

Each community agency sets its criteria for services, and once the youth meets the eligibility criteria, service delivery begins. The VR counselor is available to coordinate VR services with services provided by employment-related programs, such as youth programs funded by the U.S. Department of Labor (DOL) and provided at American Job Centers.

UNITED STATES DEPARTMENT OF LABOR YOUTH PROGRAMS

Youth programs funded under Title I of the Workforce Innovation and Opportunity Act (WIOA) include five new program elements: financial literacy instruction, entrepreneurial skills training, provision of local labor market and employment information, activities that help youth transition to postsecondary education and training, and education offered concurrently with workforce preparation activities and training for a specific occupation or occupational cluster.

Two well-known youth programs funded by the DOL are the Job Corps and YouthBuild. Each of these programs integrates vocational (including classroom and practical experiences), academic, and employability skills training designed to prepare youth for stable, long-term, high-paying employment. Job Corps programs offer career technical training in over 100 career areas. YouthBuild programs focus on the construction trades.

SOCIAL SECURITY ADMINISTRATION WORK PROGRAM

The Social Security Administration (SSA) funds the Ticket to Work program to provide career development services to beneficiaries between ages 18 and 64 to assist these individuals to become financially independent. The SSA issues a letter, referred to as the "Ticket," to eligible beneficiaries that can be used to obtain free employment services from a provider of their choice that is registered with the SSA.[2]

---

[2] "A Transition Guide to Postsecondary Education and Employment for Students and Youth with Disabilities," U.S. Department of Education (ED), August 24, 2020. Available online. URL: https://sites.ed.gov/idea/files/postsecondary-transition-guide-august-2020.pdf. Accessed February 8, 2024.

Part 5 | Living with Learning and Developmental Disabilities

Chapter 22 | Transitioning to Adulthood

Chapter Contents
Section 22.1—Addressing Social and Emotional Needs....................176
Section 22.2—Self-Determination for Youth with Disabilities..............179
Section 22.3—Making Informed Choices 183

Section 22.1 | Addressing Social and Emotional Needs

It is important to address the social and emotional needs of students with disabilities to ensure that they have the skills needed to be successful in a postsecondary educational setting or workplace. Students with disabilities who have well-developed social skills are more likely to be able to successfully navigate employment, community, and postsecondary education settings.

The Individualized Education Program (IEP) teams need to take active steps to provide opportunities for students with disabilities to acquire appropriate social skills. Many of these opportunities can be integrated into the student's existing course of study. Specific strategies include the following:

- **Role-playing.** Schools can create opportunities for students with disabilities to practice appropriate social skills in a variety of contexts, including school-based, workplace, community, and postsecondary educational settings.
- **Participation in social and emotional learning programs.** A variety of specific social skill development programs exist that can help students acquire critical social skills.
- **Positive school climate.** Parents should be aware that a positive school climate is critical to helping students with disabilities develop strong social skills. For example, safe and supportive classrooms build on the students' strengths.

PROVIDING THE STUDENT AND YOUTH WITH SUPPORT TO MAKE THEIR DECISIONS

Beyond developing social skills, it is crucial for students with disabilities to understand and acquire the skills for self-determination during high school to ensure success in postsecondary education and the workplace. Students with strong self-advocacy skills who understand and fully participate in the development of their IEP and summary of performance have better transition outcomes. Key characteristics of self-determination are the ability to:

- speak for yourself (self-advocacy)
- solve problems

- set goals
- make decisions
- possess self-awareness
- exhibit independence

Developing self-determination and making informed choices heighten students' knowledge of the transition process and success in postschool settings.

Self-determination activities can be described as activities that result in individuals with developmental disabilities, with appropriate assistance, having the ability, opportunity, authority, and support (including financial support) to:

- communicate and make personal decisions
- communicate choices and exercise control over the type and intensity of services, support, and other assistance the individual receives
- control resources to obtain needed services, support, and other assistance
- participate in, and contribute to, their communities
- advocate for themselves and others, develop leadership skills through training in self-advocacy, participate in coalitions, educate policymakers, and play a role in the development of public policies that affect individuals with developmental disabilities[1]

SOCIAL AND EMOTIONAL LEARNING

Positive social and emotional development and learning in the early years provide an important foundation for lifelong learning and development, including mental health. Building social and emotional learning every day starts with relationships and supportive learning environments. Once in place, all children can learn social skills (such as friendship skills), emotional literacy, self-regulation, and problem-solving. Teaching social skills and fostering emotional literacy can also prevent behaviors that are challenging to adults.

---

[1] "A Transition Guide to Postsecondary Education and Employment for Students and Youth with Disabilities," U.S. Department of Education (ED), August 24, 2020. Available online. URL: https://sites.ed.gov/idea/files/postsecondary-transition-guide-august-2020.pdf. Accessed February 7, 2024.

The Head Start Early Learning Outcomes Framework (ELOF): Ages Birth to Five (https://eclkc.ohs.acf.hhs.gov/interactive-head-start-early-learning-outcomes-framework-ages-birth-five) describes the skills, behaviors, and knowledge that programs must foster in all children. The Effective Practice Guides provide information about domain-specific teaching practices that support children's development.

Relationships

Responsive and positive relationships are the foundation for learning. Relationships between children and education staff, education staff and families, and children and families are important and support children's social and emotional development. Secure, consistent, and trusting relationships help children feel comfortable learning new social and academic skills and strategies.

Supportive Environments

Consistent, predictable, and supportive environments create a safe and secure place for all children to learn. Supportive environments promote engagement for every child. These environments provide consistent and predictable routines, clear expectations for what is going to happen, and developmentally appropriate choices, so children are ready to learn.

Social and Emotional Skills

Children develop social and emotional skills throughout childhood. When children learn social and emotional skills at an early age, it helps them have stronger skills for a lifetime. Building in social and emotional learning every day creates many opportunities for education staff and families to teach and model social and emotional skills. Friendship skills, emotional literacy, self-regulation, anger management, and problem-solving are all skills children can learn and practice.

Behavior Support and Challenging Behavior

Behavior has meaning. Children often exhibit behaviors that can be challenging to adults when they do not have the words or skills to let others know what they want or need. Teaching social and emotional skills can help children efficiently use words and actions to get their needs met.[2]

Section 22.2 | Self-Determination for Youth with Disabilities

Educators, vocational rehabilitation (VR) professionals, and families must engage students with disabilities in secondary transition services. Secondary transition is more successful when students take part in the planning process. Successful secondary transition planning includes the following:
- high expectations for students
- a student-centered approach
- social-emotional behavioral learning support
- supported decision-making
- respecting the student, family, and their informed decisions

SELF-DETERMINATION

An excellent way to promote high expectations, increase independence, and improve social-emotional learning is through the teaching of self-determination skills.

Self-determination and self-advocacy skills improve decision-making, goal-setting, problem-solving, self-monitoring, and self-regulation. In teaching self-determination skills, it is important to embrace diversity and to take into consideration cultural differences and nuances.

When given opportunities early, students with disabilities can develop and master the self-determination, self-advocacy, and decision-making skills critical to success in their daily activities and in their Individualized Education Program (IEP) meetings.

---

[2] "Social and Emotional Learning," Early Childhood Learning and Knowledge Center (ECLKC), October 17, 2022. Available online. URL: https://eclkc.ohs.acf.hhs.gov/teaching-practices/article/social-emotional-learning. Accessed February 7, 2024.

STUDENT PARTICIPATION IN THE INDIVIDUALIZED EDUCATION PROGRAM PROCESS

Meaningful student participation in the IEP process is just one way to help students practice and build self-determination skills. Research suggests that the following practices are important to bolster students' capacities to set their own goals and develop the abilities to achieve them:

- Ensure IEPs are aligned with the challenging academic content standards.
- Provide students with disabilities access to rigorous coursework, career and technical education, and vocational rehabilitation to explore preemployment transition services and career interests and to inform IEPs and transition planning.
- Implement the specially designed instruction noted in students' IEPs and assistive technology, related services, and other accommodations or support the student needs to make meaningful progress toward being prepared for their postsecondary goals.
- Ensure that school personnel have the tools, resources, and support to develop and implement IEPs with fidelity.

SUPPORTING STUDENTS WITH DISABILITIES

When supporting students with disabilities, schools and partnering state VR agencies should use effective practices, such as:

- fostering self-determination
- social and emotional learning programs
- self-advocacy instruction
- workplace readiness experiences
- independent living skills practice

Supporting students with disabilities and providing them with resources to make informed choices is crucial for them to make their own decisions. Self-determination means that students can speak for themselves, solve problems, set goals, make decisions, possess self-awareness, and demonstrate independence.[3]

TIPS FOR YOUTH IN TRANSITION

As a young person, you may be starting to think about your future—the kinds of things you want to do in life and the steps you can take to achieve these goals. It is an exciting time, but it can also be scary and challenging to understand your interests, learn about the different paths you can take, and make decisions under pressure. Some mistakes along the way are normal for everyone, but preparation and planning can really help.

The word "transition" is often used to refer to the period of preparation and decision-making that leads youth to successfully move from school to work. Though the paths they choose might look different, all youth should have access to transition planning and meaningful input in planning for their future career and life goals. This means you are not alone if you have questions or concerns, as talking with peers who are also thinking about their futures can help.

As you are thinking and talking with others, it is important to include everyone in the conversation about transition planning. This, in part, encourages all youth to share experiences and discuss solutions, but it can especially benefit some youth who face more significant barriers, such as youth in foster care or the juvenile justice system, disconnected youth, and youth with disabilities. For example, talking about transition planning can benefit youth with disabilities and other interested peers as they learn to recognize and navigate the barriers they may face. Whatever challenges come your way, talking about transition planning with others is a great way to learn from different perspectives and figure out a plan that best meets your individualized needs.

---

[3] "Student-Led Decision-Making in Schools," U.S. Department of Education (ED), October 31, 2023. Available online. URL: https://sites.ed.gov/osers/2023/10/student-led-decision-making-in-schools. Accessed February 7, 2024.

The Role of Self-Determination

Along with having access to conversations about transition planning comes the related idea that all youth, including youth with disabilities, should learn and practice an important skill called "self-determination." If you have not heard of self-determination before, it refers to the skills you need in order to have control over your life. Self-awareness, goal-setting, and problem-solving are three examples that can empower you to make informed decisions and achieve success—however you choose to define it—in transition. While it is an important part of transition planning, self-determination is a skill you can acquire over time and is one that you will use throughout your life, including when accessing accommodations in the workplace or expressing your interests, needs, and preferences in other ways.

Now You Are Ready to Dive In

Now that you know what transition means and about the importance of self-determination in this process and throughout your life, it is a good time to begin doing your own planning. One helpful resource for getting the conversation started is the Guiding Your Success Tool (www.ncwd-youth.info/guiding-your-success). All youth, including youth with disabilities, can use this resource to think about and answer some important elements that help contribute to success in transition. By following this tool, youth can:

- learn to set and carry out educational goals
- engage in career development, including self-exploration, career exploration, and career planning and management, in order to select education and training for the career of your choice
- participate in essential youth development activities such as mentoring, service, leadership, and other forms of community engagement to build skills such as self-advocacy and self-determination
- learn about important support to maintain physical and mental health and access to transportation, housing, benefits, and financial planning

- consider the important role of family and other caring adults in setting high expectations for all youth, including those with disabilities, throughout the process

As you practice self-determination when planning for transition, what comes next is up to you. Just remember, it is always a good idea to seek advice from peers and other caring adults along this journey of preparing your goals and making them a reality.[4]

Section 22.3 | Making Informed Choices

The vocational rehabilitation (VR) agency must provide its participants with the opportunity to exercise informed choice throughout the VR process, including making decisions about the following:
- employment goals
- services and service providers
- settings for employment and service provision
- methods for procuring services

The VR agency assists participants by providing information, guidance, and support to make and carry out these decisions. The exercise of informed choice involves communicating clearly, gathering and understanding information, setting goals, making decisions, and following through with decisions. VR counselors provide information through various methods of communication that are helpful to a family in order to assist with identifying opportunities for exercising informed choice from the beginning of the VR process through the achievement of an employment outcome.

---

[4] "Transition Planning and Self-Determination for Youth with Disabilities," Youth.gov, September 4, 2018. Available online. URL: https://engage.youth.gov/resources/transition-planning-and-self-determination-youth-disabilities. Accessed February 7, 2024.

PARAMETERS OF INFORMED CHOICE

While the Rehabilitation Act emphasizes the importance of the individual's, including the student's or youth's, ability to exercise informed choice throughout the VR process, it requires the VR agencies to ensure that the availability and scope of informed choice are consistent with the VR agencies' responsibilities for the administration of the VR program. Such requirements impose parameters that affect the exercise of informed choice. It is generally the responsibility of the VR counselor to inform the individual about relevant requirements and available options for developing the Individualized Plan for Employment (IPE) and exercising informed choice to ensure that the individual understands the options. As appropriate, the VR counselor encourages the participation of family members and others in the VR process.

PARENTAL CONSENT, AGE OF MAJORITY, SUPPORTED DECISION-MAKING, AND GUARDIANSHIP

Outreach to parents, family members, caregivers, and representatives plays a critical role in the transition process. For students who receive services under Part B of the Individuals with Disabilities Education Act (IDEA), states may transfer parental rights to the student when he or she reaches the "age of majority under state law," except for a student who has been determined to be incompetent under state law. The age of majority is the age that a state sets for a minor to become an adult and assume legal responsibility for himself/herself and all decisions that accompany that (e.g., financial, medical, and educational). In most states, this is age 18.

At the time a student reaches the age of majority, if parental rights have transferred to the student under state law, the school district must provide any notice required by Part B of the IDEA to both the student and the parents. Once parental rights transfer to the student, the student has the right to make his or her own educational, employment, or independent living decisions. The VR agencies conduct outreach directly to these students. The consent of the parents or an IDEA-eligible student who has reached the age of majority under state law must be obtained before personally identifiable information about the student is released to officials of participating agencies, including VR agencies that are providing or paying for transition services.

As IDEA-eligible students with disabilities reach the age of majority, they and their parents are advised to seek information to help them understand their options for making educational decisions. A student need not be placed under guardianship in order for his or her family to remain involved in educational decisions. Guardianship places significant restrictions on the rights of an individual. Students and parents are urged to consider information about less restrictive alternatives.

If state law permits parental rights under the IDEA to transfer to a student who has reached the age of majority, that student can become the educational rights holder who invites family members to participate in the Individualized Education Program (IEP) meeting. If the adult student does not want to have that role, he or she can execute a power of attorney authorizing a family member to be the educational decision-maker. Alternatively, if a student prefers not to execute a power of attorney, a supported decision-making arrangement can be established consistent with applicable state procedures, in which the parents (or other representatives) assist the student in making decisions. Unlike under guardianship, the student remains an autonomous decision-maker in all aspects of his or her life.

Families are encouraged to seek services from the parent training and information centers funded by the Office of Special Education Programs (OSEP) and parent information and training programs funded by the Rehabilitation Services Administration (RSA).[5]

---

[5] "A Transition Guide to Postsecondary Education and Employment for Students and Youth with Disabilities," U.S. Department of Education (ED), August 24, 2020. Available online. URL: https://sites.ed.gov/idea/files/postsecondary-transition-guide-august-2020.pdf. Accessed February 7, 2024.

Chapter 23 | Career Options and Supported Employment

Chapter Contents
Section 23.1—Postsecondary Employment Options........................188
Section 23.2—Intellectual Disability and the Americans with
　　　　　　　Disabilities Act 193

Section 23.1 | Postsecondary Employment Options

For more than two decades, one of the principal goals of disability policy in the United States, as it influenced special education, vocational rehabilitation (VR), and employment services nationwide, has been to improve employment opportunities for young people with disabilities as they exit secondary education programs. As noted in the Rehabilitation Act, as amended by the Workforce Innovation and Opportunity Act (WIOA), one of the primary purposes of the Rehabilitation Act is to maximize opportunities for individuals with disabilities, including individuals with significant disabilities, for competitive integrated employment.

TYPES OF EMPLOYMENT OUTCOMES AUTHORIZED UNDER THE REHABILITATION ACT

When developing the Individualized Plan for Employment (IPE), the student or youth with the disability may choose from any employment goal that meets the definition of an "employment outcome" for purposes of the VR program. This means the employment goal must be one in competitive integrated employment (including customized employment and self-employment) or supported employment. Each of these options is discussed in more detail subsequently.

Competitive Integrated Employment

Competitive integrated employment pays a competitive wage in a location where both workers with disabilities and those without disabilities (other than supervisors or individuals supporting the worker with a disability) interact on a daily basis while performing their jobs. Competitive integrated employment offers the same level of benefits for all employees, including those with disabilities, and offers the same opportunities for advancement for individuals with disabilities and those without disabilities working in similar positions.

The Rehabilitation Act emphasizes the achievement of competitive integrated employment to ensure that all individuals with disabilities, especially students and youth with disabilities served through the VR program, are provided every opportunity to achieve employment with earnings comparable to those paid to individuals without disabilities, in a setting that allows them to interact with individuals who do not have disabilities. Through the sharing of program information and coordination of joint training, VR programs and school staff can explore and identify transition-related services, such as work-based learning, dual enrollment programs, and competitive integrated employment or supported employment opportunities for students exiting school.

The WIOA amendments to the Rehabilitation Act build on this effort by emphasizing that individuals with disabilities, especially students and youth with disabilities, are given the opportunity to train and work in competitive integrated employment or supported employment. Both school and VR program staff are now responsible for providing documentation of completion of specific services and actions prior to referring a student with a disability to subminimum wage employment. School officials are responsible for providing the VR agency with documentation of completion of appropriate transition services under the Individuals with Disabilities Education Act (IDEA), consistent with the confidentiality requirements of the Family Educational Rights and Privacy Act (FERPA).

VR agencies are required to provide the youth with documentation of completion of transition services under the IDEA in addition to completion of preemployment transition services and other appropriate services under the VR program. The youth with a disability must obtain this documentation prior to starting a job at subminimum wage with an employer who holds a Section 14(c) certificate under the Fair Labor Standards Act (FLSA).

The VR agency staff is available to consult with school staff and others to share information that will enable school staff, students, and family members to better understand the medical aspects of disabilities as they relate to employment, the purpose of the VR program, how and when VR staff can best serve the employment needs of the students in the transition process, and how school staff can assist students in their preparation for VR services leading to an employment outcome in competitive integrated employment or supported employment.

Supported Employment

Supported employment refers to competitive integrated employment or employment in an integrated work setting in which individuals are working on a short-term basis toward competitive integrated employment. Supported employment services, including job coaching, are designed for individuals with the most significant disabilities who need ongoing support services because of the nature and severity of their disability in order to perform the work involved. A job coach provides intensive training and ongoing support to an individual to learn and perform job tasks at the worksite, teach and reinforce acceptable work behaviors, and develop positive working relationships with his or her coworkers. As needed, the job coach is able to develop individualized accommodation tools for use on the job, such as picture albums of the sequence of steps in a job or communication aids for individuals with speech or hearing deficits.

As the student or youth with a disability learns and demonstrates progress in these areas, the job coach decreases the support and time spent with the individual on the job. The job coach makes follow-up or check-in visits on the jobsite to determine if the individual is performing well on the job and to provide additional job coaching when job tasks change or the student or youth needs repeated training on a particular task.

Sometimes the job coach, family member, or youth will identify a coworker who can provide assistance rather than the job coach. This assistance offers natural support for the individual while working.

However, when there is no natural support available and the individual needs ongoing support services, a family member or another agency, such as developmental disabilities, Medicaid, or VR agencies, provides job coaching or other services. Other services frequently include transportation, daily living, or counseling services relating to attendance or arriving to work on time.

Ongoing support services needed by an individual to maintain a job, such as job placement follow-up, counseling, and training, are considered "extended services." These services are identified on the IPE, along with the service provider that will fund and provide these services. VR agencies may provide extended services to a youth with a most significant disability for a period of up to four years or until the youth turns 25 years old.

Customized Employment
While supported employment matches the individual with a position and trains him or her to perform the essential tasks in that position, customized employment designs or tailors job tasks to meet the individual's interests, skills, and capabilities, as well as the needs of the employer. Customized employment is accomplished by using various strategies, including:
- customizing a job description based on current employer needs or on previously unidentified and unmet employer needs
- developing a set of job duties, a work schedule and job arrangement, and specifics of supervision (including performance evaluation and review) and determining a job location
- using a professional representative chosen by the individual or, if elected self-representation, to work with an employer to facilitate placement
- providing services and support at the job location

Self-Employment
Self-employment refers to an individual working for himself or herself and being responsible for earning his or her own income from a trade or business rather than working for an employer and being paid a salary or wage.

A student or youth with a disability could choose self-employment in a particular business that matches his or her career strengths and interests. Individuals choose self-employment for many reasons, whether it is to work in or out of the home in order to meet family care responsibilities, to control work schedules, or to meet their accessibility needs. The range of occupations for self-employment is vast. For example, individuals with disabilities may choose to be a self-employed certified public accountant, medical billing services provider, comic book artist, or lunch cart operator, among many other options.

The VR agencies offer services and guidance to assist a student or youth with a disability to prepare for self-employment, such as training or start-up costs for their business. Typically, the VR counselor will recommend that the individual develops a business plan that includes a market analysis supporting the self-employment venture, the individual's work role in the business, anticipated income based on local market information, identification of the support services needed, and the tools, equipment, or supplies needed and their cost. In many cases, the VR counselor refers the student or youth to local community organizations that provide technical assistance to develop the business plan or pay for the development of a business plan. The student or youth and the VR counselor will use the collected information to identify the objectives and goals of their IPE.

KNOW YOUR OPTIONS TO PLAN

A range of options is available for students to use in achieving their educational and career aspirations. Students, family members, educators, VR counselors, and other support professionals are encouraged to know about available postsecondary opportunities and services to properly plan and prepare youth with a disability for adult life.[1]

---

[1] "A Transition Guide to Postsecondary Education and Employment for Students and Youth with Disabilities," U.S. Department of Education (ED), August 24, 2020. Available online. URL: https://sites.ed.gov/idea/files/postsecondary-transition-guide-august-2020.pdf. Accessed February 7, 2024.

Section 23.2 | Intellectual Disability and the Americans with Disabilities Act

The Americans with Disabilities Act (ADA), which was amended by the ADA Amendments Act of 2008 ("Amendments Act" or "ADAAA"), is a federal law that prohibits discrimination against qualified individuals with disabilities. Individuals with disabilities include those who have impairments that substantially limit a major life activity, have a record (or history) of a substantially limiting impairment, or are regarded as having a disability.

Title I of the ADA covers employment by private employers with 15 or more employees as well as state and local government employers. Section 501 of the Rehabilitation Act provides similar protections related to federal employment. In addition, most states have their own laws prohibiting employment discrimination on the basis of disability. Some of these state laws may apply to smaller employers and may provide protections in addition to those available under the ADA.

The U.S. Equal Employment Opportunity Commission (EEOC) enforces the employment provisions of the ADA.

GENERAL INFORMATION ABOUT INTELLECTUAL DISABILITIES

An intellectual disability (formerly termed mental retardation) is a disability characterized by significant limitations both in intellectual functioning and in adaptive behavior that affect many everyday social and practical skills. An individual is generally diagnosed as having an intellectual disability when:
- the person's intellectual functioning or intelligence quotient (IQ) level is below 70–75
- the person has significant limitations in adaptive skill areas as expressed in conceptual, social, and practical skills
- the disability originated before the age of 18

"Adaptive skill areas" refer to basic skills needed for everyday life. They include communication, self-care, home living, social skills, leisure, health and safety, self-direction, functional academics (reading, writing, and basic math), and work. Individuals with severe intellectual disabilities are more likely to have additional limitations than persons with milder intellectual disabilities.

An estimated 2.5 million Americans have an intellectual disability. The majority of adults with an intellectual disability are either unemployed or underemployed despite their ability, desire, and willingness to engage in meaningful work in the community.

As a result of changes made by the ADAAA, individuals who have an intellectual disability should easily be found to have a disability within the meaning of the first part of the ADA's definition of disability because they are substantially limited in brain function and other major life activities (e.g., learning, reading, and thinking). An individual who was misdiagnosed as having an intellectual disability in the past also has a disability within the meaning of the ADA. Finally, an individual is covered under the third ("regarded as") prong of the definition of disability if an employer takes a prohibited action (e.g., refuses to hire or terminates the individual) because of an intellectual disability or because the employer believes the individual has an intellectual disability.

ACCOMMODATING PERSONS WITH INTELLECTUAL DISABILITIES

The ADA requires employers to provide adjustments or modifications—called "reasonable accommodations"—to enable applicants and employees with disabilities to enjoy equal employment opportunities unless doing so would be an undue hardship (i.e., a significant difficulty or expense). Accommodations vary depending on the needs of the individual with a disability. Not all employees with intellectual disabilities will need an accommodation or require the same accommodations, and most of the accommodations a person with an intellectual disability might need will involve little or no cost.

What Types of Reasonable Accommodations May Persons with Intellectual Disabilities Need for the Application Process?

Some persons with intellectual disabilities will need reasonable accommodations to apply and/or interview for a job. Such accommodations might include the following:
- providing someone to read or interpret application materials for a person who has limited ability to read or understand complex information
- demonstrating, rather than describing, to the applicant what the job requires
- modifying tests, training materials, and/or policy manuals
- replacing a written test with an "expanded" interview

What Specific Types of Reasonable Accommodations May Employees with Intellectual Disabilities Need to Do Their Jobs or to Enjoy the Benefits and Privileges of Employment?

The following are accommodations that employees with intellectual disabilities may need:
- reallocation of marginal tasks to another employee
- training or detailed instructions to do the job, including having the trainer or supervisor:
  - Give instructions at a slower pace.
  - Allow additional time to finish training.
  - Break job tasks into sequential steps required to perform the task.
  - Use charts, pictures, or colors.

How Does a Person with an Intellectual Disability Request a Reasonable Accommodation?

There are no "magic words" that a person has to use when requesting a reasonable accommodation. An employee simply has to tell the employer that he or she needs an adjustment or change at work because of his or her intellectual disability. A request for a reasonable accommodation can also come from a family member, friend, health professional, or other representative on behalf of a person with an intellectual disability.

Are There Circumstances When an Employer Must Ask Whether a Reasonable Accommodation Is Needed When a Person with an Intellectual Disability Has Not Requested One?

Yes, an employer has a legal obligation to initiate a discussion about the need for reasonable accommodation and to provide an accommodation if one is available and if the employer:
- knows that the employee has a disability
- knows, or has reason to know, that the employee is experiencing workplace problems because of the disability
- knows, or has reason to know, that the disability prevents the employee from requesting a reasonable accommodation

May an Employer Ask for Documentation When a Person with an Intellectual Disability Requests a Reasonable Accommodation?

Yes, an employer may request reasonable documentation where a disability or the need for reasonable accommodation is not known or obvious. An employer, however, is entitled only to documentation sufficient to establish that the employee has an intellectual disability and to explain why an accommodation is needed. A request for an employee's entire medical record, for example, would be inappropriate as it likely would include information about conditions other than the employee's intellectual disability.

When a person's intellectual disability is obvious, the employer should focus on requesting documentation that describes the limitations stemming from the disability rather than on establishing that the person, in fact, has a disability. If a person has more than one disability, an employer may only ask for information related to the disability that requires accommodation. The employer may request that a physician or an appropriate professional provide information or documentation of a person's impairment. Information about a person's functional limitations can also be obtained from nonprofessionals, such as the applicant, his or her family members, and friends.

Does an Employer Have to Grant Every Request for an Accommodation?
No, an employer does not have to provide an accommodation if doing so will be an undue hardship. Undue hardship means that providing a reasonable accommodation would result in significant difficulty or expense. An employer also does not have to eliminate an essential function of a job as a reasonable accommodation, tolerate performance that does not meet its standards, or excuse violations of conduct rules that are job-related and consistent with business necessity and that the employer applies consistently to all employees (such as rules prohibiting violence, threatening behavior, theft, or destruction of property).

If more than one accommodation would be effective, the employee's preference should be given primary consideration although the employer is not required to provide the employee's first choice of reasonable accommodation. If a requested accommodation is too difficult or expensive, an employer may choose to provide an easier or less costly accommodation as long as it is effective in meeting the employee's needs.

May an Employer Be Required to Provide More than One Reasonable Accommodation for the Same Person with a Disability?
Yes, the duty to provide reasonable accommodation is an ongoing one. Although some employees with intellectual disabilities may require only one reasonable accommodation, others may need more than one. For example, an employee with an intellectual disability may require charts or pictures to learn how to do a job and later may require additional training. An employer must consider each request for reasonable accommodation and determine whether it would be effective and whether providing it would pose an undue hardship.

Do Persons with Intellectual Disabilities Need More Supervision than Other Employees?
Not necessarily. The type and amount of supervision required for an employee with an intellectual disability will depend on the type

of job and the person's individual strengths. Although it may take longer for some individuals with intellectual disabilities to master the tasks associated with a job, with the proper training, many can perform as effectively as employees without intellectual disabilities in the same job. In other situations, supervisors may have to modify how they give instructions or communicate what needs to be done as a form of reasonable accommodation. For example, some employees with intellectual disabilities may benefit from additional day-to-day guidance or feedback or from having a large task broken down into smaller parts that are easier to understand.

CONCERNS ABOUT SAFETY

When it comes to safety, an employer should be careful not to act on the basis of myths, fears, generalizations, or stereotypes. Instead, the employer should evaluate each individual on his or her knowledge, skills, experience, and the extent to which the intellectual disability affects his or her ability to work in a particular job.

When May an Employer Refuse to Hire or Terminate a Person with an Intellectual Disability Because of Safety Concerns?

An employer may refuse to hire or terminate a person with an intellectual disability for safety reasons when the individual poses a direct threat. A "direct threat" is a significant risk of substantial harm to the individual or others that cannot be eliminated or reduced through reasonable accommodation. This determination must be based on objective, factual evidence.

HARASSMENT

The ADA prohibits harassment or offensive conduct based on disability just as other federal laws prohibit harassment based on race, sex, color, national origin, religion, age, and genetic information. Offensive conduct may include, but is not limited to, offensive jokes, slurs, epithets or name-calling, physical assaults or threats, intimidation, ridicule or mockery, insults or put-downs, offensive objects or pictures, and interference with work performance. Although the law does not prohibit simple teasing, offhand comments, or isolated incidents that are not very serious, harassment is illegal when it is so frequent or severe that it creates a hostile or offensive work environment or when it results in an adverse employment decision (such as the victim being fired or demoted).

What Should Employers Do to Prevent and Correct Harassment?

Employers should make clear that they will not tolerate harassment based on disability or on any other basis. This can be done in a number of ways, such as through a written policy, employee handbooks, staff meetings, and periodic training. The employer should emphasize that harassment is prohibited and that employees should promptly report such conduct to a manager. Finally, the employer should immediately conduct a thorough investigation of any report of harassment and take swift and appropriate corrective action.

RETALIATION

The ADA prohibits retaliation by an employer against someone who opposes discriminatory employment practices, files a charge of employment discrimination, or testifies or participates in any way in an investigation, proceeding, or litigation related to a charge of employment discrimination. It is also unlawful for an employer to retaliate against someone for requesting a reasonable accommodation. Persons who believe that they have experienced retaliation may file a charge of retaliation as described subsequently.

HOW TO FILE A CHARGE OF EMPLOYMENT DISCRIMINATION Against Private Employers and State/Local Governments

Any person who believes that his or her employment rights have been violated on the basis of disability and wants to make a claim against an employer must file a charge of discrimination with the EEOC. A third party may also file a charge on behalf of another person who believes he or she experienced discrimination.[2]

---

[2] "Persons with Intellectual Disabilities in the Workplace and the ADA," U.S. Equal Employment Opportunity Commission (EEOC), May 15, 2013. Available online. URL: www.eeoc.gov/laws/guidance/persons-intellectual-disabilities-workplace-and-ada. Accessed February 7, 2024.

Chapter 24 | Philosophy of Independent Living

Independent living is about life. It is about choice, seeing to your own affairs, and pursuing your talents, interests, passions, and selfhood as independently as possible. We all would like to see our young people grow to adulthood and find their place in the world, doing for themselves to the best of their ability.

Disability can complicate independence, to be sure, which is why independent living can be an important part of helping a young person with a disability get ready for life after high school. The more involved the disability, the more likely it is that independent living will be a subject of serious discussion—and preparation.

PHILOSOPHICAL UNDERPINNINGS

It is clear from searching the term "independent living" on the web that a great deal of passion and commitment exists in the independent living movement and community. It is rather breathtaking, in fact. You will see phrases such as all people achieving their maximum potential, barrier-free society, self-determination, self-respect, dignity, equal opportunities, consumer-driven, and empowerment. At its heart, the passion in the independent living community is fueled by individuals with disabilities themselves. This passion for selfhood is worldwide. Consider this statement found on the website of the Independent Living Institute in Sweden (www.independentliving.org/toolsforpower/tools7.html). It surely captures the point:

Independent living does not mean that we want to do everything by ourselves and do not need anybody or that we want to live in isolation. Independent living means that we demand the same choices and control in our everyday lives that our nondisabled brothers and sisters, neighbors, and friends take for granted. We want to grow up in our families, go to the neighborhood school, use the same bus as our neighbors, work in jobs that are in line with our education and interests, and start families of our own. We are profoundly ordinary people sharing the same need to feel included, recognized, and loved.

DEFINING INDEPENDENT LIVING

The Center on Transition Innovations posts the following definition of independent living:

> Independent living is defined as "those skills or tasks that contribute to the successful independent functioning of an individual in adulthood." We often categorize these skills into the major areas related to our daily lives, such as housing, personal care, transportation, and social and recreational opportunities.

Each of these areas related to our daily lives, of course, has its own aspects and concerns that the Individualized Education Program (IEP) team will want to consider and plan ahead for, as appropriate for the student's needs and plans.

DOES A STUDENT NEED TRANSITION PLANNING AND SERVICES IN THE DOMAIN OF INDEPENDENT LIVING?

It is important to understand that not all students with disabilities will need an in-depth investigation of, and preparation for, independent living after high school. As the U.S. Department of Education (ED) stated in its Analysis of Comments and Changes section (www.parentcenterhub.org/wp-content/uploads/repo_items/IDEA2004regulations.pdf):

> The only area in which postsecondary goals are not required in the IEP is in the area of independent living skills. Goals in the area of independent living are required only if appropriate. It is up to the child's IEP team to determine whether the IEP goals related to the development of

Philosophy of Independent Living | 203

independent living skills are appropriate and necessary for the child to receive free appropriate public education (FAPE).

Whether or not will very much depend on the nature and severity of the student's disability. As the ED notes, it is up to each student's IEP team to decide if planning for independent living is needed. If the IEP team feels that the student can benefit from transition planning and services in this domain, then independent living will be an area of discussion during IEP meetings where the transition is discussed.

WHAT IS INVOLVED IN INDEPENDENT LIVING?

Independent living clearly involves quite a range of activities, skills, and learning needs. Consider just the three mentioned in the definition posted at the National Secondary Transition Technical Assistance Center (NSTTAC): leisure/recreation, home maintenance and personal care, and community participation. Each of these can be broken down in its own turn to include yet more skills, activities, and learning needs. Just think about what is involved in "home maintenance and personal care" alone. It includes everything from brushing teeth to shopping for food to cooking it to cleaning up afterward, to getting ready for bed, locking the front door, and setting the alarm clock for the next day. It is a lot to keep track of, all the little facets and skills of taking care of ourselves as best we can, with support or solo.

So how an IEP team takes on the task of planning for a student's independent living in the future will depend on the nature and severity of the student's disability. Some students will not need transition planning or services to prepare for independent living. Others will need a limited amount, targeted at specific areas of need or interest. And still others, especially those with significant support needs, will need to give independent living their focused attention.[1]

---

[1] "Independent Living Connections," U.S. Department of Education (ED), March 22, 2019. Available online. URL: https://sites.ed.gov/idea/files/postsecondary-transition-guide-august-2020.pdf. Accessed February 7, 2024.

Chapter 25 | Sexuality, Relationships, and Disabilities

Chapter Contents
Section 25.1—Supporting Youth through Puberty and Adolescence.........206
Section 25.2—Talking about Sexual Health............................210
Section 25.3—Preventing and Responding to Sexual Abuse 214

Section 25.1 | Supporting Youth through Puberty and Adolescence

Adolescence is the phase of life when youth begin transitioning into adulthood. During this time, they will experience physical, sexual, social, and emotional changes caused by hormonal changes in their body. Puberty occurs during adolescence and is when a youth's body becomes physically able to have youth. For most youth, puberty begins at ages 9–14.

Youth with intellectual and developmental disabilities (IDDs) mature physically and sexually like adolescents without disabilities although sometimes the timing can differ depending on the type of disability. For example, youth with severe cognitive disabilities are more likely to experience puberty earlier than youth without these disabilities. On the other hand, many females with autism spectrum disorder (ASD) or cerebral palsy (CP) start menstruating later than their peers.

WHAT CHANGES TO EXPECT DURING PUBERTY

Here are some examples of the physical changes youth will experience during puberty:
- **females and males**:
  - growth spurts
  - body hair growth
  - excess sweating
- **females**:
  - breast growth
  - menstruation
  - vaginal discharge
- **males**:
  - enlargement of the penis and testes
  - nocturnal emissions (wet dreams)
  - involuntary erections
  - deeper voice

Social and emotional changes during puberty can include things such as the desire for more privacy and an increasing need for independence. During puberty, you might notice that your youth's feelings and expressions of those feelings are more intense. These changes might be large or small depending on the youth's developmental disability.

HOW CAN PARENTS AND CAREGIVERS HELP YOUTH WITH INTELLECTUAL AND DEVELOPMENTAL DISABILITIES NAVIGATE PUBERTY?
Overall Support
As a parent or caregiver, you can support your youth through this phase by helping them learn about puberty and what physical and emotional changes to expect. Here are some general tips when approaching puberty with your youth:
- **Use direct, anatomically correct language to avoid confusion and make youth more comfortable with all their body parts.**
- **Discuss the physical and emotional changes with your youth in early adolescence, ideally before they have experienced them.** This will give them time to think about what is going to happen and ask questions. Tell them these changes they will experience or are experiencing now are normal, and they should not be ashamed of them. If your youth tends to worry a lot, it might be good to have these discussions gradually.
- **Teach your youth about appropriate behavior in private and public spaces.** This can be a difficult concept for some youth with IDD to understand, so it is important to reinforce it. For example, always close the door when getting dressed and going to the bathroom.

Support for Physical Changes
You can help your youth feel more prepared for the physical changes they will experience during puberty. Here are some ways to help prepare both you and them for these changes:
- **Talk to your youth's doctor.** Your youth's doctor can be an important resource for both you and your youth during puberty. For example, if your youth is having a

hard time dealing with menstruation (also called their "period"), their doctor might have options to help with pain management or control the flow of menstruation. A doctor can also help address other changes during puberty, such as acne. You can also meet with a doctor before your youth goes through puberty to discuss what to expect and think about ways to help you and your youth with the physical and behavioral changes.
- **Encourage and support good hygiene.** Like their non-IDD peers, youth with IDD will likely need your help learning about new hygiene needs, such as using deodorant. In addition, females might need information about menstrual products such as pads and tampons and how to find a product they are comfortable using. Males might need information about what to do if they have a wet dream and how to take care of new body hair. All youth need to know about how their bodies are growing and changing and how to care for them as they transition into adulthood. Help youth find puberty-related products they like. It might take some trial and error to find the products that work for their bodies.
- **Work with caregivers and schools to ensure youth have accommodations to support proper hygiene with dignity.** For example, ensure youth have privacy in the bathroom, even if they need support from you or another caregiver.

Support for Social and Emotional Changes

Increasing independence and opportunities for social interaction are an important part of transitioning to adulthood. It is an exciting time, and youth with IDD might need extra help to navigate this independence and these opportunities. Here are some ways you can support your youth as they encounter the social and emotional changes of puberty:
- **Find ways for your youth to gain independence and take part in social activities.** For example, help them plan a trip to the movies with friends. With practice, youth

with IDD can gain valuable social skills such as greeting people, using eye contact and appropriate body language, respecting personal space, standing up for themselves, and understanding customs for telephone and computer use.
- **Expect some conflict and approach it calmly.** As your youth seeks more independence, your relationship with them could start to include more conflict. During puberty, some youth rebel against their parents or other caregivers, which is normal and will usually decrease over time. Parents and caregivers might have to find ways to balance their youth's privacy and independence while also keeping their youth safe. For example, you may talk to your youth about when they can have alone time in their room without being interrupted.
- **Acknowledge that youth will begin to experience sexual and romantic feelings during puberty.** Support your youth in understanding these new feelings by talking to them about healthy relationships, the qualities they might look for in a partner, consent, and boundaries. For example, you might ask your youth about what personality traits they think would make the perfect partner for them. Also, some youth with IDD may not experience feelings or emotions in the same way a youth without IDD does. As a parent, you might need to discuss feelings in a way that feels safe to your youth.[1]

---

[1] Administration for Children and Families (ACF), "Sexual Health Resource Toolkit for Parents and Caregivers of Youth with Intellectual and Developmental Disabilities," U.S. Department of Health and Human Services (HHS), January 1, 2023. Available online. URL: https://teenpregnancy.acf.hhs.gov/sites/default/files/resource-files/Sex-Toolkit-Parents-Youth-IDD.pdf. Accessed February 7, 2024.

Section 25.2 | Talking about Sexual Health

Talking honestly and openly with your kids about sex and relationships is important—and it is never too early to start. Your support can help them make healthy choices and avoid risks as they grow up. It may be hard to know where to start, especially if your parents did not talk to you about sex when you were growing up. The following tips and strategies can help.

WHAT DO YOU SAY TO YOUR CHILDREN?

Kids have different questions and concerns about sex at different ages. As your children get older, the things you talk about will change. Remember to:

- talk early and often (You do not have to fit everything into one conversation.)
- be ready to answer questions (Children's questions can tell you a lot about what they already know.)
- listen carefully to your kids' opinions (even if you do not agree)
- try using things that come up on television (TV), in music, or on social media to start a conversation
- be honest about how you are feeling (e.g., if you are embarrassed or uncomfortable, it is okay to say so)[2]

TIPS FOR TALKING TO YOUR YOUTH WITH INTELLECTUAL AND DEVELOPMENTAL DISABILITIES ABOUT SEXUAL HEALTH AND RELATIONSHIPS

Do you feel comfortable talking about sex and relationships with your youth? Do you want more guidance about how to talk to youth with intellectual and developmental disabilities (IDDs) about relationships and sex? You are not alone.

---

[2] Office of Disease Prevention and Health Promotion (ODPHP), "Talk to Your Kids about Sex and Healthy Relationships," U.S. Department of Health and Human Services (HHS), February 28, 2024. Available online. URL: https://health.gov/myhealthfinder/healthy-living/sexual-health/talk-your-kids-about-sex-and-healthy-relationships. Accessed February 29, 2024.

Sexuality, Relationships, and Disabilities

Fact
- **Many youths with IDD will eventually have romantic relationships.** They need and want information and life skills on sexual health and relationships, like any other youth their age.
- **Sometimes youth with IDD are not offered sexual health education at school.** Parents and caregivers can help fill this gap by sharing their values and expectations for how their youth can stay safe and healthy.

How Do You Start the Conversation?
Be Open
- Remind your youth that you are a safe place to discuss their questions about sex and relationships.
- **You do not have to know it all.** If you do not know the answer to a question or are not ready to talk about it right then, make eye contact and tell them that you will get more information and follow up.

Practice a Positive Approach
- Use eye contact and open body language, such as a relaxed but attentive posture leaning slightly in, to the youth. If eye contact is difficult for your youth, as it often is for youth with IDD, try talking while you are in the car or on the couch watching TV, when the youth can focus their eyes elsewhere.
- Use simple, concrete words and concepts. For example, use the correct terms for body parts (e.g., penis and vagina) instead of slang terms.
- Give verbal cues such as "okay" and "uh huh" to show you are listening.
- Try to stay calm and take a deep breath before responding to a question or comment.
- Occasionally say, "tell me what you understand..." to make sure they have the same understanding about terms and concepts as you.
- Repeat back and paraphrase to show you want to understand, using phrases such as, "What I hear you saying is...."

What Is Important to Talk About?
- physical and emotional development, including puberty
- expectations about what it means to be in a healthy romantic relationship, such as how to decide and communicate what you want and need (what consent or "saying yes" looks like and how to give and get consent before sexual activity)
- setting boundaries in relationships to stay safe and healthy (Teach them to respect other people's boundaries.)
- how to access sexual health services, such as where to get contraception and/or human immunodeficiency virus (HIV)/sexually transmitted infection (STI) testing

Conversation Starters
- Do you hope to be in a relationship one day?
- What kinds of fun activities would you like to do with a romantic partner?
- What are some characteristics you are looking for in a romantic partner?
- Do you think you will get married one day?
- Do you want to have youth? Why or why not?

Discuss Your Values and Hopes for Them
Communicate your values about relationships and sexuality but realize that your youth may hold different values.

Talk about Pregnancy and Sexually Transmitted Infection Prevention
- **Talk about how a pregnancy or STI could affect your youth.** Use simple language to help youth understand what it is like to be pregnant, give birth, and raise a youth.
- **There are many safe and effective methods to prevent unintended pregnancy and STIs.** Some methods are more effective and easier to use than others. You and your youth can talk with a medical professional about the method that might work best.

Things You Can Do
- **Include your youth when deciding whether birth control is appropriate now.** Openly discuss the birth control options with your youth and their doctor.
- **Remember that only the correct and consistent use of condoms prevents STIs.** Condoms and contraception should be used together every time someone has sex to avoid unintended pregnancy and STIs. Your medical provider may be able to demonstrate correct condom use.

Some Final Tips
Find a Copilot
- Engage another adult caregiver in your youth's life, such as your partner, a health-care provider, or your youth's teacher, to support your efforts to communicate openly and honestly about sex and relationships. Make sure they are giving similar messages about sexual health as you are.
- Model healthy relationships in your home with your family and friends, so your youth can learn what healthy relationships look like through example.
- Many schools, religious institutions, or community-based groups offer relationship and sexual health education to supplement what you are discussing at home. Typically, these programs offer a variety of approaches to help align with your family's values.

Use the Moments You Have
- Some parents and caregivers find it helpful to use situations about dating, love, or sex that come up while watching TV or listening to the radio in the car.
- **Talk about sexual health and relationships a little bit at a time.** It is important for parents and caregivers to cover topics more than once to make sure their youth understands. Conversations about sexual health are not a one-time conversation. There is not one time when you give "the talk." Instead, think of these evolving conversations as ongoing, starting in early adolescence and continuing into adulthood.

- If your youth is attending a course on sexual health, you can ask your youth to "teach you" what they learned and listen without judgment. Ask specific questions. Instead of, "How was your school class today?" say, "Tell me one thing you learned in your 'learning about my body' class today."[3]

Section 25.3 | Preventing and Responding to Sexual Abuse

Sexual abuse can happen to anyone, including youth with intellectual and developmental disabilities (IDDs). Sexual assault is sexual contact or behavior that occurs without the explicit consent of the victim. In fact, youth with IDD are at a higher risk of sexual abuse than youth without IDD. They are also less likely to report assault to parents and caregivers, as well as the police.

One reason might be that youth with IDD might have increased dependence on adults. They might not be able to understand or communicate what is happening to them. They might also have less access to sexuality education at school.

HOW YOU CAN HELP PREVENT ABUSE
Talk to Your Youth

- Talk with your youth in a developmentally appropriate way about personal safety and consent.
- Help youth understand that some parts of the body are private, and people should not look at or touch them. Tell them that they have a right to decide who touches their bodies.
- Identify which caregivers or medical staff may touch areas typically covered by a bathing suit with their permission and the situations when they may need to do this. Also, mention that youth can ask to have someone else in the room with them during medical exams.

[3] Administration for Children and Families (ACF), "Sexual Health Resource Toolkit for Parents and Caregivers of Youth with Intellectual and Developmental Disabilities," U.S. Department of Health and Human Services (HHS), January 1, 2023. Available online. URL: https://teenpregnancy.acf.hhs.gov/sites/default/files/resource-files/Sex-Toolkit-Parents-Youth-IDD.pdf. Accessed February 6, 2024.

- Help your youth identify what makes them uncomfortable. Emphasizing to them what is and is not appropriate behavior will help them know when it is abuse.
- Remind them that it is okay to politely say no even to non-sexual touching, such as hugs.
- Discuss what to do when using the restroom when you are outside the home, such as:
  - using public restrooms independently if possible
  - closing and locking bathroom or stall doors
  - restricting nudity to appropriate spaces such as a bathroom, bedroom, or changing room in a locker room
- Let your youth know they can talk to you about anything, even if someone told them to keep something a secret or private.

Advocate for Your Youth
- **Understand that most youth are abused by someone they know and trust.** Avoid focusing exclusively on "stranger danger" or the idea that assault is only perpetrated by someone the youth does not know.
- **Evaluate the caregivers who care for your youth.** For example, contact multiple references, conduct a background check, and drop in unexpectedly when they are providing care.
- **Seek educational opportunities on sexual health outside the home.** Make sure that your youth learns basic facts about sex.

PARENTS AND CAREGIVERS MIGHT BE ABLE TO RECOGNIZE SIGNS OF ABUSE IN THEIR YOUTH

Recognizing sexual assault and ongoing sexual abuse can be more difficult in youth who are nonverbal or otherwise cognitively delayed. Parents can look for new or more frequent self-stimulatory behaviors, such as repetitive movements or sounds (known as "stimming"), and new or more frequent behaviors leading to self-injury.

Some Signs of Abuse or Assault
- Physical signs are difficulty sitting or walking, bruises or pain in genital areas, headaches, stomach aches, or sexually transmitted diseases.

- Behavioral signs are depression, substance abuse, withdrawal, avoiding specific settings or people, sleep or appetite changes, crying spells, seizures, phobias, regression, guilt or shame feelings, self-destructive behavior, feelings of panic, sexually inappropriate behaviors, severe anxiety or worry, resists physical exams, learning difficulties, irritability, or a change in habits or moods.

Look for repeated or multiple signs since these signs can also appear in youth who are not being abused. For example, a youth might feel depressed or have headaches due to another reason than abuse.

Youth might or may not disclose abuse to you. If they do, it could happen by telling you directly or indirectly by mentioning something like "a friend told me…." You can support your youth by:
- believing them
- never blaming them
- providing a safe environment
- reassuring them that they did nothing wrong[4]

---

[4] Administration for Children and Families (ACF), "Sexual Health Resource Toolkit for Parents and Caregivers of Youth with Intellectual and Developmental Disabilities," U.S. Department of Health and Human Services (HHS), January 1, 2023. Available online. URL: https://teenpregnancy.acf.hhs.gov/sites/default/files/resource-files/Sex-Toolkit-Parents-Youth-IDD.pdf. Accessed February 7, 2024.

Part 6 | Additional Resources

Chapter 26 | Directory of Organizations Providing Support for People with Learning and Developmental Disabilities

Agency for Healthcare Research and Quality (AHRQ)
5600 Fishers Ln.
7th Fl.
Rockville, MD 20857
Phone: 301-427-1104
Website: www.ahrq.gov

Americans with Disabilities Act (ADA)
U.S. Department of Justice
Disability Rights Section
950 Pennsylvania Ave., N.W.
Washington, DC 20530-0001
Toll-Free: 800-514-0301
TTY: 833-610-1264
Website: www.ada.gov

Center for Parent Information and Resources (CPIR)
570 Broad St.
Ste. 702.
Newark, NJ 07102
Phone: 973-642-8100
Website: www.parentcenterhub.org

Centers for Disease Control and Prevention (CDC)
1600 Clifton Rd.
Atlanta, GA 30329-4027
Toll-Free: 800-CDC-INFO
(800-232-4636)
Toll-Free TTY: 888-232-6348
Website: www.cdc.gov

Resources in this chapter were compiled from several sources deemed reliable; all contact information was verified and updated in April 2024.

ChildCare.gov
330 C St., S.W.
4th Fl., Mary E. Switzer Bldg.
Washington, DC 20201
Toll-Free: 800-422-4453
Phone: 202-690-6782
Website: https://childcare.gov
Email: ChildCare.gov@acf.hhs.gov

Eunice Kennedy Shriver National Institute of Child Health and Human Development (NICHD)
P.O. Box 3006, Rockville, MD 20847
Toll-Free: 800-370-2943
Phone: 301-496-5133
Toll-Free Fax: 866-760-5947
Website: www.nichd.nih.gov
Email: NICHDInformation ResourceCenter@mail.nih.gov

Federal Communications Commission (FCC)
45 L St., N.E.
Washington, DC 20554
Toll-Free: 888-225-5322
Phone: 202-418-1122
Toll-Free Fax: 866-418-0232
Website: www.fcc.gov

Genetic and Rare Diseases Information Center (GARD)
P.O. Box 8126
Gaithersburg, MD 20898-8126
Toll-Free: 888-205-2311
Website: https://rarediseases.info.nih.gov

InsureKidsNow.gov
7500 Security Blvd.
Baltimore, MD 21244
Toll-Free: 877-543-7669
Website: www.insurekidsnow.gov

MedlinePlus
8600 Rockville Pike
Bethesda, MD 20894
Toll-Free: 888-FIND-NLM (888-346-3656)
Phone: 301-594-5983
Website: www.medlineplus.gov

National Highway Traffic Safety Administration (NHTSA)
1200 New Jersey Ave., S.E.
W. Bldg.
Washington, DC 20590
Toll-Free: 888-327-4236
Phone: 202-366-4000
Toll-Free TTY: 877-561-7439
Website: www.nhtsa.gov
Email: nhtsa.webmaster@dot.gov

National Institute of Mental Health (NIMH)
6001 Executive Blvd.
MSC 9663
Bethesda, MD 20892-9663
Toll-Free: 866-615-6464
Website: www.nimh.nih.gov
Email: nimhinfo@nih.gov

National Institute of Neurological Disorders and Stroke (NINDS)
P.O. Box 5801
Bethesda, MD 20824
Toll-Free: 800-352-9424
Website: www.ninds.nih.gov

Directory of Organizations | 221

National Institute on Aging (NIA)
P.O. Box 8057
Gaithersburg, MD 20898
Toll-Free: 800-222-2225
Toll-Free TTY: 800-222-4225
Website: www.nia.nih.gov
Email: niaic@nia.nih.gov

National Institute on Deafness and Other Communication Disorders (NIDCD)
31 Center Dr., MSC 2320
Bethesda, MD 20892-2320
Toll-Free: 800-241-1044
Phone: 301-827-8183
Toll-Free TTY: 800-241-1055
Website: www.nidcd.nih.gov
Email: nidcdinfo@nidcd.nih.gov

National Institutes of Health (NIH)
9000 Rockville Pike
Bethesda, MD 20892
Phone: 301-496-4000
TTY: 301-402-9612
Website: www.nih.gov
Email: olib@od.nih.gov

U.S. Department of Education (ED)
400 Maryland Ave., S.W.
Washington, DC 20202
Toll-Free: 800-USA-LEARN
(800-872-5327)
Phone: 202-401-2000
Website: www.ed.gov

U.S. Department of Health and Human Services (HHS)
200 Independence Ave., S.W.
Hubert H. Humphrey Bldg.
Washington, DC 20201
Toll-Free: 877-696-6775
Website: www.hhs.gov

U.S. Department of Labor (DOL)
200 Constitution Ave., N.W.
Washington, DC 20210
Toll-Free: 866-4-USA-DOL
(866-487-2365)
Website: www.dol.gov

U.S. Department of Transportation (DOT)
1200 New Jersey Ave., S.E.
Washington, DC 20590
Toll-Free: 855-368-4200
Phone: 202-366-4000
Website: www.transportation.gov

U.S. Equal Employment Opportunity Commission (EEOC)
131 M St., N.E.
Washington, DC 20507
Toll-Free: 800-669-4000
Toll-Free TTY: 800-669-6820
Website: www.eeoc.gov
Email: info@eeoc.gov

U.S. Social Security Administration (SSA)
1100 W. High Rise
6401 Security Blvd.
Baltimore, MD 21235
Toll-Free: 800-772-1213
Toll-Free TTY: 800-325-0778
Website: www.ssa.gov

INDEX

Index

Page numbers followed by "n" refer to citation information; by "t" indicate tables; and by "f" indicate figures.

A

AAP *see* American Academy of Pediatrics
accommodations
   Individualized Education Program (IEP) 135, 180
   intellectual disability 196
   nonverbal learning disability (NVLD) 65
   overview 143–148
ADHD *see* attention deficit hyperactivity disorder
Administration for Children and Families (ACF)
   publications
      preventing and responding to sexual abuse 216n
      sexual health 214n
      supporting youth through puberty and adolescence 209n
Agency for Healthcare Research and Quality (AHRQ), contact information 219
American Academy of Pediatrics (AAP)
   autism spectrum disorder (ASD) 76
   developmental screening 8, 113
Americans with Disabilities Act (ADA), contact information 219

anxiety
   fragile X syndrome (FXS) 104
   language and speech disorders 48
   nonverbal learning disability (NVLD) 66
   sexual abuse 216
AOS *see* apraxia of speech
APD *see* auditory processing disorder
apraxia of speech (AOS), speech and language development 12
ASD *see* autism spectrum disorder
assistive technology
   auditory processing disorder (APD) 54
   early intervention 117
   Individualized Education Program (IEP) 180
   postsecondary education 168
   special education 146
   vocational rehabilitation (VR) services 152
attention deficit hyperactivity disorder (ADHD)
   auditory processing disorder (APD) 53
   dysgraphia 37
   fetal alcohol spectrum disorders (FASDs) 94
   overview 69–72
   see also autism spectrum disorder (ASD)
auditory processing disorder (APD)
   language and speech disorders 47
   overview 52–55
   see also visual processing disorders

225

autism spectrum disorder (ASD)
   developmental screening 8
   fragile X syndrome (FXS) 104
   language and speech disorders 48
   overview 73–78
   puberty and adolescence 206
   see also attention deficit
      hyperactivity disorder (ADHD)

B

birth defects
   Down syndrome 108
   overview 85–89
brain development
   brain architecture and learning 13
   fragile X syndrome (FXS) 103
brain injury
   attention deficit hyperactivity
      disorder (ADHD) 70
   dyslexia 33
   language and speech disorders 47

C

Center for Parent Information and
   Resources (CPIR)
   contact information 219
   publications
      accommodations for students
         with disabilities 146n
      early intervention 125n
      Individualized
         Education Program (IEP)
         139n, 140n, 141n
      special education 136n
      vocational rehabilitation (VR)
         services 148n, 151n,
         158n, 162n
Centers for Disease Control and
   Prevention (CDC), contact
   information 219
cerebral palsy (CP)
   overview 79–83
   puberty 206
child development, overview 113–116

childcare, child development 116
ChildCare.gov
   contact information 220
   publication
      child care options 116n
childhood vaccines
   brain development 15
   hearing loss 100
CIE *see* competitive integrated
   employment
cognitive development
   early intervention services 119
   overview 4–7
competitive integrated
   employment (CIE)
   postsecondary employment
      options 188
   vocational rehabilitation (VR)
      services 160
CP *see* cerebral palsy

D

developmental delay
   auditory processing
      disorder (APD) 53
   autism spectrum disorder (ASD) 76
   early intervention strategies 117
   fragile X syndrome (FXS) 104
developmental language
   disorder (DLD)
   speech disorder 12
   see also specific language
      impairment (SLI)
developmental milestones
   autism spectrum disorder (ASD) 73
   cognitive development 6
   language and speech disorders 48
Diagnostic and Statistical Manual
   of Mental Disorders, Fifth
   Edition (DSM-5)
   fetal alcohol spectrum
      disorders (FASDs) 93
   nonverbal learning
      disability (NVLD) 64

Index | 227

DLD *see* developmental language disorder

Down syndrome
  autism spectrum disorder (ASD) 74
  birth defects 86
  developmental delay 122
  overview 106–109
  see also fragile X syndrome (FXS)

DSM-5 *see* Diagnostic and Statistical Manual of Mental Disorders, Fifth Edition

dyscalculia
  educational interventions 129
  learning disabilities 20
  overview 41–44
  see also dyslexia

dysgraphia
  educational interventions 129
  learning disabilities 20
  overview 37–39

dyslexia
  educational interventions 128
  learning disabilities 20
  overview 33–36
  visual processing disorders 56
  see also dyscalculia

dyspraxia, overview 59–62

E

Early Childhood Learning and Knowledge Center (ECLKC) publications
  early brain development and health 18n
  early cognitive development 5n
  social and emotional learning 179n

early intervention strategies, overview 117–125

educational interventions, overview 127–129

EEO *see* Equal Employment Opportunity

epilepsy, birth defects 87

Equal Employment Opportunity (EEO), intellectual disability 193

Eunice Kennedy Shriver National Institute of Child Health and Human Development (NICHD)
  contact information 220
  publications
    Down syndrome 109n
    dyscalculia 42n
    learning disabilities 24n, 25n, 129n

F

Fair Labor Standards Act (FLSA), postsecondary employment 189

Family Educational Rights and Privacy Act (FERPA), postsecondary employment 189

FAPE *see* free appropriate public education

FAS *see* fetal alcohol syndrome

FASDs *see* fetal alcohol spectrum disorders

Federal Communications Commission (FCC), contact information 220

FERPA *see* Family Educational Rights and Privacy Act

fetal alcohol spectrum disorders (FASDs), overview 91–95

fetal alcohol syndrome (FAS)
  birth defects 88
  early intervention strategies 122
  see also Down syndrome

FLSA *see* Fair Labor Standards Act

fragile X syndrome (FXS)
  autism spectrum disorder (ASD) 74
  early intervention strategies 122
  overview 103–106

free appropriate public education (FAPE)
  high school diploma 165
  independent living 203

free appropriate public
   education (FAPE), *continued*
   Individuals with Disabilities
      Education Act (IDEA) 136
FXS *see* fragile X syndrome

G
Genetic and Rare Diseases
   Information Center (GARD),
   contact information 220

H
hearing loss
   birth defects 86
   overview 97–100
   speech and language
      development 11, 47
   see also vision loss
hyperlexia, reading disorders 30

I
IDDs *see* intellectual and
   developmental disabilities
IDEA *see* Individuals with Disabilities
   Education Act
IEE *see* Independent Educational
   Evaluation
IEP *see* Individualized Education
   Program
IFSP *see* Individualized Family Service
   Plan
Independent Educational
   Evaluation (IEE), special education
   and related services 133
Individualized Education
   Program (IEP)
   Down syndrome 108
   educational interventions 128
   high school education and training
      opportunities 164
   independent living 202
   nonverbal learning
      disability (NVLD) 65

response to intervention (RTI) 25
social and emotional needs 176
visual processing disorders 58
Individualized Family Service
   Plan (IFSP), described 123
individualized plan for
   employment (IPE)
   accommodations for students 147
   overview 158–162
   postsecondary employment
      options 188
Individuals with Disabilities Education
   Act (IDEA)
   cerebral palsy (CP) 83
   Down syndrome 108
   dyslexia 34
   early intervention strategies 117
   nonverbal learning
      disability (NVLD) 64
   overview 136–137
   vocational rehabilitation (VR)
      services 150
InsureKidsNow.gov, contact
   information 220
intellectual and developmental
   disabilities (IDDs)
   learning disability 20
   sexual health 210
intelligence quotient (IQ)
   dysgraphia 39
   fetal alcohol spectrum
      disorders (FASDs) 92
   nonverbal learning
      disability (NVLD) 63
IPE *see* individualized plan for
   employment
IQ *see* intelligence quotient

L
language and speech disorders,
   overview 46–49
least restrictive environment (LRE),
   educational interventions 127
LRE *see* least restrictive environment

Index | 229

M

MedlinePlus
  contact information 220
  publications
    Down syndrome 108n
    dyslexia 36n
    trisomy X 110n

N

National Center on Birth Defects and Developmental Disabilities (NCBDDD)
  publications
    attention deficit hyperactivity disorder (ADHD) 72n
    autism spectrum disorder (ASD) 74n
    birth defects 85n
    brain development 15n
    cerebral palsy (CP) 83n
    child development 115n
    developmental monitoring and screening 10n
    early cognitive development 7n
    fetal alcohol spectrum disorders (FASDs) 95n
    fragile X syndrome (FXS) 106n
    hearing loss in children 100n
    intellectual disability 90n
    language and speech disorders in children 49n
    vision loss in children 101n
National Highway Traffic Safety Administration (NHTSA), contact information 220
National Human Genome Research Institute (NHGRI)
  publication
    genetic disorders 103n
National Institute of Mental Health (NIMH)
  contact information 220
  publication
    autism spectrum disorder (ASD) 78n
National Institute of Neurological Disorders and Stroke (NINDS)
  contact information 220
  publication
    developmental dyspraxia 60n
National Institute on Aging (NIA), contact information 221
National Institute on Deafness and Other Communication Disorders (NIDCD)
  contact information 221
  publications
    congenital anomalies 86n
    specific language impairment (SLI) 52n
    speech and language developmental milestones 12n
National Institutes of Health (NIH), contact information 221
NIH News in Health
  publication
    hearing and vision loss 102n
nonverbal learning disability (NVLD), overview 62–66
NVLD *see* nonverbal learning disability

O

occupational therapy
  dysgraphia 39
  early intervention 118
  support and accommodations for students 145
Office of Disease Prevention and Health Promotion (ODPHP)
  publications
    early childhood development and education 4n
    sex and healthy relationships 210n

P

phenylketonuria (PKU)
   birth defects 86
   brain architecture and
     learning 15
physical therapy
   early intervention 118
   nonverbal learning
     disability (NVLD) 66
PKU *see* phenylketonuria
postsecondary education
   education and training
     opportunities 164
   support and accommodations for
     students 146
preterm birth
   cerebral palsy (CP) 81
   developmental screening 8
   visual processing disorders 56

R

reading disorders, overview 30–32
response to intervention (RTI),
   diagnosing learning disability 24
RTI *see* response to intervention

S

school psychologists
   diagnosing learning disability 25
   vocational rehabilitation (VR)
     services 154
SLI *see* specific language impairment
special education service
   child development 114
   diagnosing learning disability 24
   educational interventions 127
   language and speech
     disorders 48
specific language impairment (SLI)
   overview 49–52
   see also developmental language
     disorder (DLD)
speech and language development,
   overview 10–12

speech therapy
   cerebral palsy (CP) 82
   developmental dyspraxia 62
   fragile X syndrome (FXS) 105
speech-language pathologists
   developmental monitoring,
     screening, and evaluation 9
   diagnosing learning disability 25
   language and speech disorders 48
supplementary aids and services,
   Individualized Education
   Program (IEP) 138

T

toxic stress, brain architecture
   and learning 17
transition planning
   independent living 203
   out-of-school youth 171
   vocational rehabilitation (VR)
     services 153
triple X syndrome, overview 109–110

U

U.S. Department of Education (ED)
   contact information 221
   publications
     decision-making in schools 181n
     impact of dyspraxia 59n
     independent living
       connections 203n
     Individuals with Disabilities
       Education Act (IDEA) 137n
     postsecondary education and
       employment for students
       170n, 172n, 177n, 185n, 192n
U.S. Department of Health and
   Human Services (HHS), contact
   information 221
U.S. Department of Labor (DOL),
   contact information 221
U.S. Department of
   Transportation (DOT), contact
   information 221

U.S. Equal Employment Opportunity
    Commission (EEOC)
    contact information 221
    publication
        intellectual disability and the
            ADA 199n
U.S. Social Security
    Administration (SSA), contact
    information 221

V
vision loss
    overview 100–102
    see also hearing loss
visual processing disorders
    overview 55–59
    see also auditory processing
        disorder (APD)
vocational rehabilitation (VR) services
    accommodations for students 147
    overview 150–158

VR see vocational rehabilitation
    services

W
WIOA see Workforce Innovation and
    Opportunity Act
Workforce Innovation and
    Opportunity Act (WIOA),
    out-of-school youth 172

X
x-ray, birth defects 87

Y
Youth.gov
    publication
        transition planning and self-
            determination for youth with
            disabilities 183n